D0336425

Gardening in a Cold Climate

Mrs North's entertaining and instructive book describes her adventures in gardening under rather difficult conditions during the past 25 years. Her own garden is situated in a frost pocket near a Yorkshire town and the plants growing there have to overcome both industrial grime and long periods of low temperatures.

From these experiences Mrs North has been able to make planting suggestions for the rock garden, herbaceous border, shrub border, woodland and ground cover. Bulbs, roses and climbing plants are all included and Mrs North does not forget those who garden on acid soils and those who enjoy the beauty and variation of foliage.

Her enthusiasm for, and enjoyment of, gardening are self-evident on every page and throughout the book she gives sensible and practical advice.

Gardening in a Cold Climate

FELICITY NORTH

W. H. & L. COLLINGRIDGE LTD
LONDON

DEDICATION

To my husband and fellow toiler

First published in 1967
by W. H. & L. Collingridge Ltd
Tower House, Southampton St., W.C.2
Made and printed in Great Britain
by William Clowes and Sons Ltd
London and Beccles

Contents

Illustrations

PHOTOGRAPHS

LINE DRAWINGS

by G. R. Kingbourn

Acknowledgements

I would like to thank Mr. F. Swallow for looking over the manuscript, attending to my syntax, and giving me such helpful advice. I would also like to acknowledge with thanks permission to quote as follows: Messrs W. Heinemann Ltd – an extract from 'Crisis' by Christopher Hassall ; the Literary Trustees of Walter de la Mare and The Society of Authors as their representative, for an extract from a poem by Walter de la Mare from the book *English Poetry* by Kenneth Hopkins; Messrs Penguin Books Ltd – an extract from *A Selection* by Matthew Arnold edited by Kenneth Allott; Messrs Sidgwick & Jackson – an extract from 'The Old Vicarage, Grantchester', in the *Collected Poems* of Rupert Brooke; and Messrs Metheun and Co Ltd, – an extract from 'Fires', by Joseph Campbell.
I am grateful to Mr Bernard Alfieri, Mr A. J. Huxley and Mr H. Smith for providing me with photographs.

Introduction

How various his employment, whom the world
Calls idle; and who justly in return
Esteems that busy world an idler too!
Friends, books, a garden and perhaps his pen,
Delightful industry enjoyed at home
And nature in her cultivated trim,
Dressed to his taste, inviting him abroad—
Can he want occupation who has these?

W. Cowper

For as long as I can remember I have loved the country. I was born in London, of Kentish stock, and some of my happiest childhood memories are centred upon Epping Forest and Regent's Park. I can remember feeding the squirrels in the Park regularly, and the delight I felt when they ran along my arm for their nuts; being taken to the Zoo, and the unforgettable smell of damp autumn leaves.

When I was nine the family came to Yorkshire, to an old grey stone house with about four acres of land. At last I had returned to the land, to the sights and smells of the countryside.

Time moved on. I met the man with whom I was to share my life and was given the choice of living either in the country or the town. I had always wanted a large garden, so my decision was not a difficult one to make. I married and became the joint possessor of a plot of land set amid the Yorkshire coalfields.

This plot slopes from west to east and was originally just over half an acre in extent. A farm field of rather more than an acre flanked it to the north, and we were lucky enough to be able to include this in our property 25 years ago.

At the foot of the garden runs a tributary of the River Ouse. When we first came to live here there were trout in the stream and the occasional flash of the kingfisher could be seen.

An undulating hill rises at the other side of the stream, and I remember thinking that I could be happy with such a background for the rest of my days. A row of pylons now runs along the top of my dream hill and the once peaceful countryside is now being relentlessly swallowed up by houses. The air is no longer still, but hums with the throb of farm tractors and the sound of builders' hammers. No longer are the evenings dark and peaceful. Lights blaze along our country lanes, lights glitter through the trees. This is 'progress'. We draw our curtains and silently pray that some of our countryside in these industrial areas may be preserved.

Our plot of land is low-lying, so catching every ground frost in the British Isles. It is a dry plot and one which receives, when the wind is blowing east, a daily shower of carbon from the coke ovens two miles away. The soil is a heavy neutral clay, beneath which a layer of shale runs unevenly, as a result of which the trees bow to the prevailing westerly winds. Experienced gardeners would never choose to live in places such as this. It is an area in which pessimists say nothing will grow. And yet, looking back, I see it as a wrestling ring, in which every setback is a challenge to get up and try again.

It is nearly 30 years since we settled here and my memory is becoming as short as some of my experiments have been. I have recollections of our small red brick house being surrounded by endless privet hedges, spotted laurels and 'rustic' rose arches, of lawns studded with thousands of dandelions and of fruitful hours spent on my knees, stabbing each weed to the heart with a knitting needle dipped in concentrated sulphuric acid. Potting shed, greenhouse and garage were strewn around the house with reckless abandon, so that the view from each window comprised either a building or a privet hedge. One by one, over long periods of time, these were removed to more satisfactory situations.

There had been an attempt by the previous owner of the house to lay out a garden. A lawn had been levelled to the rear of the house, the surplus soil having been thrown up to form a rock garden, on the top of which a privet hedge had been planted. Beyond the lawn a narrow border had been made, with marguerites and Michaelmas daisies, and, beyond that, a miscellaneous collection of fruit trees had been put in. A quickthorn hedge divided this half acre from the farm field on the left, through which we had a right of way to the road at the bottom. The house faced the village green and our drive to the road across it was by courtesy of the then Lord of the Manor. It was important, therefore, that our right of way across the farm field should be maintained, so all coal and similar heavy goods were diverted this way, to the complete mystification of the purveyors.

Now there is a copse where once there was a field, wide stretches of lawn and thousands of plants which have chosen to stay with us.

Each spring myriads of bulbs greet us as they thrust enquiring heads above the soil. Each spring the frosts bow down the daffodils, whose buds lie, like large limp green tadpoles, on the surface of the hoar-encrusted soil. Most of them rise again, but the flowers of others hang, face downwards, on frost-fractured stems, and each spring, for the past few seasons, the buds of forsythia and ornamental cherry dapple the earth, discarded by the destructive bullfinches.

It has not been my intention to choose a likely spouse for an aspiring lady gardener. Should you want a nice large garden to walk in but not work in, then marry a millionaire. If such an ambition be impossible of achievement then, ladies, face any intended prospect squarely and select him as you would select a race-horse, bearing the following points in mind. Is he too tall? No good, his back will give out. Is he too thin? Constitutionally unfitted for wheeling heavy wheel-barrows, mixing concrete, lawn mowing, hedge cutting and the sundry other duties he will be required to perform. Is he generous? He will have to be, so that your own extravagant tastes, in the way of purchases for the garden, may be indulged and glossed over. And will he mind your doing all the nicer bits of gardening, the selection of material, the planning and the planting? Will he mind when you take all the credit for having a lovely garden? And will he be annoyed when he catches you trying to roll out with a rolling pin the footprints that you have inadvertently made in his ever-wet concrete? Will he mind having a wife with coal-heaver's shoulders, wearing one of his cast-off mackintoshes reaching to her ankles, and having a head-hugging hat atop wispy wind-knotted hair? Surely not, although there are moments of doubt when, in passing, he growls, 'You'd hardly make a glamour queen.'

In this book I have tried as far as is possible to give the common names of plants, where they exist, in addition to the Latin botanical ones; but the question of names has always been a stumbling block to the beginner, and, indeed, the botanists themselves often find difficulty in making clear-cut divisions between some families of plants. For example, among the prunus, or Plum family may be found, as well as plums:

Almonds	*P. amygdalus*
Apricots	*P. armeniaca*

Bird Cherry	*P. padus*
Cherries	*P. cerasus*
Cherry Laurel	*P. laurocerasus*
Peaches	*P. persica*
Portugal Laurel	*P. lusitanica*

and the following may still be found occasionally in nursery lists under the pyrus, or Pear family:

Crab Apples	*Malus*
Chokeberries	*Aronia*
Japanese Quince	*Chaenomeles*
Mountain Ash and Whitebeam	*Sorbus*

When referring to the Latin names of plants, it will be found that the first one applies to the genus. The second name belongs to the species and the last one, if there are more than two, belongs to the variety. This last name often denotes a variation from the species in colour of flower or foliage, or a form often named after the person by whom it was introduced. Thus in the case of *Cotinus coggygria atropurpureus:*

Cotinus	= the genus, or family
coggygria	= the species or member of the family
atropurpureus	= the variety.

I hope that this explanation will be of help to readers in understanding catalogue descriptions.

As a final point, of which gardeners are aware, the seasonal growth of trees and shrubs varies from year to year, but an attempt at accuracy has been made in the lists at the ends of the chapters. In some cases the rates of growth given in these are at variance with the remarks in the text. This may be explained by the occurrence of winter 'die-back' which can be severe in some years. It is also extremely difficult to estimate the ultimate height of trees which take many years to reach maturity, and I have, in such cases, relied on the experience of recognised authorities.

But let us proceed. The stage is set. Let us now bring on the characters.

CHAPTER ONE

Evergreens

And I must work thro' months of toil,
And years of cultivation,
Upon my proper patch of soil
To grow my own plantation.

Tennyson

When planting a garden, the first subjects to consider are the evergreens. Unfortunately, in an area of heavy atmospheric pollution, the possibilities among evergreen trees and shrubs are extremely limited, so much so that when I am asked to recommend suitable ones for the district my brain ceases to function.

When I look round the countryside in my immediate vicinity, I can see nothing in the way of a 'prosperous' evergreen; 'stunted' is the only adjective to describe them. Most of those growing in this area lose a proportion of their foliage during the winter, that is, if they can stand the conditions at all. These include escallonia, holly, privet, pyracantha, and the evergreen members of the cotoneaster and berberis families. The most fully evergreen plants are the conifers, and they often brown badly, due to the icy winter winds.

The Blue Atlantic Cedar, *Cedrus atlantica glauca*, put in 25 years ago, has achieved about 6 inches of new growth a year. When the fresh needles grow in the spring you can just get a glimpse of what this tree should really look like. It rapidly acquires a more sombre hue, but cedars have wonderful outlines and are well worth planting for this reason alone. I am still waiting for this one to bear its magnificent cones, but so far it has produced only male catkins. I was interested to see that the young specimens growing at Kew were behaving similarly.

At the same time as this tree was put in, I planted the Indian Cedar, *C. deodora*, but it succumbed to the first harsh winter. Possibly it might have survived had it been protected for a few years until it had grown above ground frost level. I have seen some of these trees growing a few miles away, but do not think that cedars as a whole are fitted for industrial areas. Some established specimens of the Cedar of Lebanon, *C. libani*, possibly the best-known of all the cedars, which are growing on the fringe of our nearest industrial town, are showing distinct signs of 'going back', and it seems only a matter of time before they eventually give up altogether.

The most rapidly growing conifer planted during the past few years has been the Serbian Spruce, *Picea omorika*. This tree is making at least a foot of growth annually and it is said to be a slender spire when mature, an additional recommendation for a small garden. I have great hopes of the Serbian Spruce and am raising some plants from seed.

The Norway Spruce or Christmas Tree, *P. abies*, the Blue Spruce, *P. pungens glauca* and its variety *kosteriana*, and the Colorado White Fir, *Abies concolor*, have been most unsatisfactory, growing both slowly and untidily. This may be due to the extremely low rainfall here as well as atmospheric pollution.

I gaze in wonder at the magnificent False Cypresses, or chamaecyparis, that grow in other parts of the country. Some of those planted when the garden was first started are barely 12 feet high: *Chaemaecyparis lawsoniana allumii*, Triomphe de Boskoop, *fletcheri*, *glauca* Spek, take your choice. In this grime they all look the same colour. *C. l. lutea*, a golden one, seems to grow as well as any of the *lawsoniana* hybrids, but I fancy that the *C. pisifera* forms can stand the climate better, as there is quite a fair specimen of the Sawara Cypress, *C. p. plumosa aurea*, growing in rough grass. Encouraged, I put in another small plant of this variety in the open ground a few years ago, and it is already more than 6 feet high.

Among the smaller growing chamaecyparis, *lawsoniana ellwoodii* seems to stand the wind better than its slightly more feathery-foliaged relative, *C. l. fletcheri*, which is an extremely dainty silvery conifer, but needs a fairly sheltered position, otherwise it browns badly on the windward side. Both of these are sometimes recommended for rock gardens and, admirable subjects as they are for this purpose when small, it must be remembered that they ultimately reach a height of about 15 feet. My specimens grow at the rate of about 6 inches a year, which is as much as the taller growing varieties.

Another small conifer, which started life here as a rock garden specimen, has done so well that I feel it would be quite satisfactory for a small garden. This is another variety of the Sawara Cypress, *C. p. squarrosa*. At about 5 feet high, with a spread of 3 feet, its glaucous

A view of the author's garden. A sloping bank divides the lawns and in a yew enclosure a seat provides rest for the weary

The author's garden: the large lawn which fronts the copse. On the left is *Cedrus atlantica glauca*

Above: *Mahonia japonica* has heavily perfumed sprays of lemon-yellow flowers which appear in February and March

Right: The graceful Weeping Birch, *Betula pendula youngii*

juvenile foliage is most attractive. Planted in a sheltered spot it came through the unusually severe winter of 1962 completely unharmed.

The Irish yew, *Taxus baccata fastigiata*, can almost be termed a dwarf conifer in my part of Yorkshire. It grows slowly, probably making 3 or 4 inches of new wood a year, but withstands the cold and smoke much better than the chamaecyparis. A plant put in over 20 years ago, about a foot in height, has now reached about 9 feet. The form *T. b. fastigiata aurea* is of even slower growth.

As an experiment, 10 years ago I purchased three specimens of *Libocedrus decurrens*, or Incense Cedars. These are lovely trees of fastigiate habit, with a quite exceptional depth of colour and, when you brush against the foliage, a most delicious scent. My first three trees died immediately and were replaced by smaller specimens. These were getting on fairly well until the winter of 1962, not the worst in our experience here, but the worst since they were introduced into the garden. The combination of low temperatures and icy winds killed much of the growth, but the plants themselves did not die. I cut off the dead wood and they are now recovering but have not yet thickened up.

One of the more successful conifers is the Western Arbor-vitae, *Thuja plicata*. It is withstanding the dirty conditions well, growing moderately quickly. This tree is often recommended for blocking out unsightly objects and it will do this, although of late years I have noticed that the density has decreased as the height has increased. It is said to make a tremendous specimen, but this will not concern gardeners living in the coalfields, not, at any rate, in their lifetime.

Thinking that the thujas had solved all my evergreen tree problems, I planted a specimen of *T. occidentalis fastigiata* several years ago. Alas and alack, it has been most disappointing, growing slowly and looking thoroughly dissatisfied.

Both the Austrian Pine, *Pinus nigra austriaca*, and the Scots Pine, *P. sylvestris*, refuse to co-operate and remain quite small specimens, putting on no more than 4 inches of new growth a year.

Of the larger, or should I say taller growing, junipers, *Juniperus chinensis* is doing well and I should say may be a good choice for an industrial garden, as so far it does not seem to brown on the windward side, nor yet die back in patches. Encouraged, I have recently planted a specimen of Young's Golden Juniper, *J. c. aurea*. This is said to attain a height of 13 to 15 feet and is certainly a wonderful colour, but my plant is still only 12 inches high.

Many years ago one of my kind friends gave me a cutting of *J. squamata meyeri*. It now stands about 5 feet tall, but the most handsome silver-blue foliage is only really dazzling when the tree is making its new growth. In cleaner atmospheres it is the same sparkling silver as the Koster's Spruce, *Picea pungens kosteriana*, but even bluer in tone.

A matching pair of the Irish Juniper, *J. communis hibernica*, that I bought for the purpose of flanking a short flight of steps, has not been successful. The two trees grew unequally and one looked so very awful that I pulled it up. Although this juniper is considered to be one of the hardiest species, I have not found it so. The specimen that I disposed of, although not actually dead, was badly browned on one side, while a tree growing in a local garden, in an exposed position, died completely during a hard winter. On the other hand, *J. virginiana glauca*, a silvery-foliaged variety of the Pencil Cedar, not so slim in growth, is still alive but growing slowly.

I had seen some magnificent trees of the Western Hemlock, *Tsuga heterophylla*, at Sheffield Park in Sussex, so I thought I would like to try one or two near the stream in the bottom of the garden, as I had read that they liked a moist soil. They were growing slowly until the winter of 1962, which finished one of them off completely and left the other with about one piece of living foliage. I grew the Eastern Hemlock, *T. canadensis*, from seed a few years ago, but got rid of the plants before they had time to disappoint me. Obviously the climate here is too dry for these trees.

So far I have only dealt with the tall growing or fastigiate evergreens, but there are many positions in the garden where a large prostrate plant can be introduced with advantage. The Creeping Juniper, *J. horizontalis*, is one of these. The one in our garden covers the site of an erstwhile fish pond.

Years ago, we made a pool and planted it according to the book. That was before the age of plastics and fibreglass. It was only a matter of time before the sides cracked, due to subsidence, and the pool leaked. Every winter, when the pond froze over, we used to have to break the ice to see how the fish were faring and check the level of the water, adding more if necessary. It was an unpalatable chore and one that was usually left undone for as long as possible.

In one particularly hard winter, my husband went away and I was instructed to keep the hole in the ice open and see that the water had not drained away. It was exceptionally cold and the ice was thick. The day before his return I 'remembered' to look. Horrors! All the water had vanished and there, on their sides in the black mud at the bottom of the pool, gazing at me with an unwinking one-eyed stare, were the goldfish. Noticing the expression of reproach in their upturned eyes, I hastily got a net and removed the bodies to a bucket full of water, where they immediately started swimming about in an ecstasy of abandon.

At one time I was given sundry overgrown goldfish-bowl fish for my pool by various members of my family, but after this incident was reported, I was told I was not fit to have them!

Later, I essayed an aquarium of tropical fish, the 'expert' advice decreeing that the inmates should be fed on live food to keep them healthy. Daily I visited the stream at the bottom of the garden, net in one hand, jar in the other and, with gumboots awash, filtered the sand from the river bed through my net. And what a collection! There were millions of worms. Red ones, white ones, things with tails, tubifex, shrimps and endless multitudes of wriggling larvae. Encouraged by the ease with which I obtained all this fresh food for my fish, I persuaded one of my friends to take over while I went on holiday. For hours she fished about in the mud abortively, then one of the neighbours called, to whom she retailed her plight. 'Why,' said the neighbour, 'can't you find any then? She seems to get plenty. Let me have a try.' So she, too, entered the stream but, alas, unsuccessful also, sank into its uncharted depths. Describing her experience to her husband later she was horrified at the lack of sympathy shown by the irrelevance of his response. 'Ee, Elsie love,' he said, 'I do wish you would try to talk more posh.'

But to get back to the low-growing junipers. Another easy one is the Prostrate Juniper, *J. communis depressa*, and its golden-toned relative, *J. c. d. aurea*. The new growth of the first has, or do I imagine it, the peculiar habit of half turning its tips, so that it looks as though it is twisting itself preparatory to passing through the eye of a needle. *J. c. d. aurea* does not do this, but it is much admired and is used to conceal the stump of a cherry tree cut down several years ago. Both of these varieties of the Prostrate Juniper cover quite a lot of ground, but at least they are really prostrate. I think they are better used as dot plants rather than planted in small rock gardens. All junipers have an aromatic perfume which I like.

The complaints about the growth of evergreens in this part of the world have been loud and long. These plants are a test of patience for me as I am well aware that even when they do survive they are extremely poor specimens and, in the words of my oldest friend, would be 'far better gone'.

Do not be discouraged, though. Perhaps you will have better luck than I. It is most important that you should try to grow some of them in your garden if it is to look furnished during the winter months.

As I have already mentioned, there were here when we came several plants of the Variegated or Spotted Laurel, *Aucuba japonica variegata*. This is a shrub that will thrive anywhere, even in heavy shade and, as with the holly, bears berries only on female plants. If you dislike it on account of its having spots, or because it is too common, there are plain-leaved forms which have the same merits. *A. j. viridis* is the commonest of these, and there is one named *A. j. hillieri*, with attractive dark green leaves and large red berries.

Another shrub which will withstand shade, and one which also bears berries only on the female plants, is *Skimmia japonica*. This does not make a tall bush for it rarely exceeds 3 to 4 feet in height. Forms of *S. japonica* include *foremanii*, which is a hybrid combining both sexes and therefore berrying. The species *S. reevesiana* is also hermaphrodite. If you already have in your garden some specimens of *S. japonica* which are not berrying at all, it might be as well to introduce a male form, such as *S. j. fragrans*. Do not expect large plants of any of these from the nurseryman. The ones usually sent out are rarely more than 12 inches high and take several years to reach sizeable proportions.

And what, you may ask, is wrong with the good old English holly, *Ilex aquifolium*? Nothing, except that even this is partly defoliated in the worst of our winters and is parsimonious in the extreme in the production of its berries. The holly is among those plants botanically termed dioecious, meaning that male and female flowers are borne on separate plants. To make things more confusing, the female hollies have masculine names and the males, feminine ones. There is in the garden a variegated specimen named *I. a.* Silver Queen, which is said to be a gentleman. Whether or not I was sent the wrong variety I do not know, but my plant bears the occasional bunch of berries. To help conceal the depths of its shame, the blackbirds hasten to eat them as soon as they become conspicuous.

Of course, you may prefer to grow a golden-variegated holly, say *I. a.* Golden Queen, or one with yellow berries, such as *I. a. pyramidalis fructu-luteo*. They are all perfectly hardy, although extremely slow growing in the initial stages.

The most freely berrying holly is said to be *I. a. pyramidalis*, but whether this is so or not I shall never know, as the birds devour all the berries in the garden and when I want any I have to rely upon artificial ones.

I was absolutely enchanted when I first saw the Calico Bush, *Kalmia latifolia*, with its charming pink bells, and was determined to possess one. I did, but in spite of every care and attention it has resolutely refused to bear a single flower for the whole of the 15 years of its life here. At first, I planted it in light shade with no result, but after reading that sometimes it did not flower in the shade and might do better in the sun, I put it in a more open position. After five years it is still without a sign of a bloom, but I have not yet pulled it up as it is only a small shrub and makes a neat little evergreen, flowers or no flowers.

I give a rather hollow laugh when I hear people enthusing about camellias, saying that they are perfectly hardy and will grow practically anywhere, given the right soil conditions. This is not to say that I do not enthuse myself when I see them doing well, but have any of these enthusiasts ever seen these lovely plants growing in industrial areas *in the open*? Gone are the scintillating green leaves: they are a dull sludgy colour; the flower buds brown at the slightest hint of frost, and it takes literally ages to produce a 3-foot plant from a nursery specimen. Over the last six or seven years I have made abortive efforts to establish one or two of these difficult plants, and I believe the answer must lie in growing them in pots under glass until the wood is sufficiently hard for them to stand the low outside winter temperatures here. I see the odd specimen existing in one or two more elevated local gardens, and would love to own a thrifty plant of, say, Donation. But, in any event, the double forms of these beautiful flowers would never command 100 per cent of my admiration, as they suffer from that irremediable complaint of 'being an unconscionable time a'dying', the old brown blooms remaining on the bushes to detract from the effect of the fresh new ones.

I am prepared to agree with what most gardening writers say about the berberis family, but these shrubs, as such, leave me cold. This personal feeling is possibly due to the fearsome spines on their branches, and you will find, in my comments on Roses on page 126, that I take the same view of these thorny subjects. Let me make my case plain. Since I sat down on, or tripped over, call it what you will, a rose species many years ago, my attitude towards anything with prickles has been distinctly uncompromising. I do not like them in the garden. Now the berberis family is probably supreme in this respect, and I cannot remember ever either working near a bush or picking the berries for floral arrangements without almost becoming impaled.

However, of the evergreens, *Berberis darwinii* and *B. stenophylla* produce lovely floral displays in the spring. When first I saw *B. darwinii* I was fascinated by the masses of orange-yellow flowers and begged a root from my neighbour. It has never looked quite the same in my garden, and I believe it must have realised that my fickle heart has changed, for over the past few years the bush has become smaller and smaller.

We are enjoined to plant *B. stenophylla* as an impenetrable hedge, and I will second that. It is impenetrable, and very handsome when full grown, but no mention is made of the fact that it suckers like mad, creeping for yards beyond its allotted space. To divide a small garden between two houses with a hedge of this plant would, I am certain, cause 'neighbour trouble' in no time at all.

A quickthorn hedge runs round my garden and we had thought this impenetrable too, until the day a full-grown bull walked through it on to the front lawn. So terrified am I of these huge and nasty brutes that I rushed to close my backdoor, locked it and ascended the stairs at the double. I am sure no bull would have ever managed to stroll casually through a hedge of *B. stenophylla*. Both these barberries are large shrubs and require plenty of room.

There is a third berberis species in the garden by the name of *verruculosa*. This is a smaller plant altogether, strictly non-invasive, and growing slowly into a compact little bush.

Nearly everyone recognises the Holly-leaved Berberis, or *Mahonia aquifolium*, once called *Berberis aquifolium*. This is almost indispensable in town gardens for winter effects and propagates itself freely from seed. We have to wash the leaves when required for Christmas decoration, but it is most useful for this purpose. It bears its sweetly scented deep yellow flowers in terminal sprays quite early in the spring, and these are followed by clusters of purplish berries, hence its further name of Oregon Grape.

A finer shrub altogether is *M. japonica*. The leaves are also pinnate but of a lighter shade of green and the whole bush, of looser habit of growth, has a most aristocratic bearing. Its heavily perfumed sprays of lemon-yellow flowers appear in February and March and it is a real treasure. Mahonias dislike being moved, so that it is better to plant them at once in their permanent places. They prefer shade, and one of the finest specimens I have ever seen is growing locally under a silver birch tree, in a moist position adjacent to a farmyard where it receives plenty of good food. It is not too difficult to layer.

While I am discussing winter-flowering evergreens, you will probably be interested in my experiences with the Laurustinus, *Viburnum tinus*. I have tried this in the garden on several occasions but with no luck at all, as it is definitely not hardy here and invariably succumbs to a hard winter. Not so its relative, *V. rhytidophyllum*. This is a tall, handsome shrub with long, dark green, wrinkled leaves. In the spring it bears clusters of white flowers rather like those of the elderberry, and these are followed by red fruits turning to black. Single specimens do not fruit freely so that it is advisable to plant more than one bush. Now when this viburnum likes its situation it can be very handsome, but with me it seems to spend its entire life with the leaves at half mast, rather like a rhododendron suffering from cold and drought in the winter. Of its hardiness there can be no doubt, but I think it would be as well to examine local specimens as to behaviour before filling up an important place in the garden with it.

On heavy soil I have found it preferable to plant evergreen trees and shrubs in the spring rather than in the autumn, as fewer losses are then liable to occur. If this is done, however, it is most important to keep an eye on your plants in times of spring drought, seeing that they have plenty of moisture and occasional overhead spraying.

PLANTS REFERRED TO IN THIS CHAPTER

Name	*Origin of species*	*Ultimate height*	*Description*	*Annual rate of growth in author's garden*
Abies concolor	Rocky Mts. of S. Colorado, Mexico to New Mexico and Arizona	100ft.	The Colorado White Fir.	3–4in.
Aucuba				
japonica variegata		6–9ft.	The common Variegated Laurel. All aucubas thrive in the shade.	
hillieri		6–9ft.	Large lustrous green leaves. Crimson berries.	
viridis		6–9ft.	Vigorous, unspotted.	

Name	*Origin of species*	*Ultimate height*	*Description*	*Annual rate of growth in author's garden*
Berberis				
darwinii	Chile	6–12ft.	Orange flowers in May.	12–24in.
stenophylla		10ft.	Orange flowers in May. Very vigorous and prickly.	12–24in.
verruculosa	China	4–6ft.	Useful small evergreen. Makes a dome-shaped bush.	12–24in.
Camellia Donation		Probably not more than 6ft. in my part of Yorkshire	Large, semi-double, pink.	
Cedrus atlantica glauca		Up to 90ft.	The Blue Cedar. One of the noblest of conifers with blue-grey glaucous foliage. Needs a great deal of space.	6–9in.
deodora	W. Himalaya	Up to 100ft.	The Himalayan Deodar. A most beautiful tree of pendent habit.	
libani	Lebanon and Syria	70–100ft.	The Cedar of Lebanon. Grows slowly into a picturesque tree, with the leading shoot bent over at the tip.	
Chamaecyparis				
lawsoniana	S.W. Oregon N.W. California	Up to 70ft.		
allumii		30–40ft.	Glaucous grey pyramidal form.	6–9in.
ellwoodii		15ft.	Slow-growing variety with glaucous blue foliage.	4–9in.
fletcheri		12–15ft.	Forms glaucous blue feathery pyramids.	4–6in.
glauca Spek		30–35ft.	Grows quite quickly but looks rather dull in the winter.	9–12in.
lutea		30–50ft.	An attractive golden form.	6–9in.
Triomphe de Boskoop		40–50ft.	Beautiful glaucous blue.	6–9in.

Name	*Origin of species*	*Ultimate height*	*Description*	*Annual rate of growth in author's garden*
Chamaecyparis				
pisifera plumosa aurea		20–30ft.	The golden-leaved form of the Sawara Cypress. Keeps its foliage better in my part of Yorkshire than the *lawsoniana* varieties.	6–9in.
squarrosa		8ft.	Feathery glaucous foliage which seems impervious to frost and smog. Makes a dense bush.	6–9in.
Ilex aquifolium				
Golden Queen		15–20ft.	Leaves broadly margined bright gold. Male.	6–9in.
pyramidalis		15–20ft.	Considered to be the finest berrying form.	9–18in.
fructu-luteo		15–20ft.	Golden berries.	
Silver Queen		15–20ft.	Leaves with creamy-white marginal variegation. Male.	6–9in.
Juniperus				
chinensis	China, Mongolia, Japan	25–30ft.	The Chinese Juniper. Hardy and wind resistant.	9–12in.
aurea		13–15ft.	Young's Golden Juniper. Beautiful golden foliage.	3–6in.
communis depressa		prostrate	Low spreading habit.	6–12in.
aurea			Young growths tinged bronzy-yellow.	6–9in.
communis hibernica		20ft.	Slim columnar habit. Glaucous foliage.	6–9in.
horizontalis	N. America	prostrate	The Creeping Juniper with glaucous foliage. Roots as it runs. Handsome and hardy but requires plenty of room.	6–9in.
squamata meyeri		6–8ft.	Erect shrub of dense habit. Foliage a lovely blue-grey.	3–4in.
virginiana glauca		Up to 50ft.	Silvery foliage.	3–6 in.
Kalmia latifolia	Eastern N. America	10ft.	The Mountain Laurel or Calico Bush. Lovely pink flowers in May/June.	4–6in.

Name	*Origin of species*	*Ultimate height*	*Description*	*Annual rate of growth in author's garden*
Libocedrus decurrens	Oregon to lower California	50–70ft.	The Incense Cedar. Glossy green foliage, stiff columnar habit.	9–12in.
Mahonia aquifolium	Western N. America	6ft.	The Holly-leaved Berberis. Yellow flowers in April/May followed by glaucous blue berries. Good in shade.	6in.
japonica	Japan	6ft.	Handsome pinnate foliage. Gloriously scented lemon-yellow flowers in February/March.	12–18in.
Picea				
abies	Central and N. Europe	60 to 100ft.	The Christmas Tree. Inclined to lose the lower branches early in life.	6–9in.
omorika	Yugoslavia	Up to 80ft.	Narrow pyramidal tree. Rapid growth. The most satisfactory Spruce yet tried.	12–24in.
pungens glauca		80ft.	The Colorado Spruce. Of rather untidy growth in this area.	6–12in.
kosteriana		30–40ft.	A wonderful shade of blue but quite impossibly slow-growing in my part of Yorkshire.	
Pinus nigra				
austriaca		Up to 80ft.	The Austrian Pine. Dark green leaves. Rather a depressing tree.	4–6in.
sylvestris	Europe and N. Asia	70–120ft.	The Scots Pine. Bark of the mature trees is of orange or reddish colour.	4in.
Skimmia				
foremanii		3ft.	Hermaphrodite form.	3–6in.
japonica	Japan	3–4ft.	Shade-bearing shrub bearing berries on the female plant.	3–6in.
fragrans		3ft.	Male form.	
reevesiana	China	2ft.	Hermaphrodite form.	3–6in.

Name	Origin of species	Ultimate height	Description	Annual rate of growth in author's garden
Taxus baccata				
fastigiata		40ft.	The Irish Yew. Slow-growing fastigiate tree.	3–9in.
aurea		35ft.	Golden form, even more slow growing.	3–4in.
Thuja				
occidentalis fastigiata		40ft.	The upright form of the Northern White Cedar.	3–4in.
plicata	W. North America	80ft.	The Western Red Cedar. Useful for blocking out unsightly objects. Very hardy.	9–12in.
Tsuga				
canadensis	E. North America	70ft.	The Eastern Hemlock.	3–4in.
heterophylla	W. North America	80ft.	The Western Hemlock.	3–4in.
Viburnum				
rhytidophyllum	China	10–20ft.	Flowers dull yellowish-white in May. Berries red, then black.	9–12in.
tinus	S.E. Europe	6–12ft.	Laurustinus. Flowers white, pinkish in bud, December/April.	

CHAPTER TWO

On Deciduous Trees and Other Plants

The unpolitical and steady trees
Tufted about our country never care
What hourly crises prickle in the air:
They borrow their opinions from the breeze.

Christopher Hassall

When we plant evergreens, we plant the 'bones' of the garden but we also need leaf-losing trees to lighten the effect.

When they start a new garden, most people seem to be able to acquire a stock of seedling silver birches, or *Betula pendula*, and nothing will give greater pleasure than a small copse planted with these trees. To provide a contrast in the winter to their silvery-white trunks, a few bushes of the Red-barked Dogwood, or *Cornus alba*, look well sprinkled among them. The dogwood eventually forms a self-layering thicket of twigs about 8 feet tall, casts its leaves in the autumn in a crimson blaze, in contrast to the clear yellow of the silver birches, and retains, on its bare twigs, terminal clusters of white, wax-like berries to delight the flower arranger. This is the ordinary dogwood, but there is a better variety called *C. a. sibirica*, the Westonbirt Dogwood, which I think I should try were I beginning again. A less well-known birch, quite suitable for the small garden, is the graceful weeping form, *B. p youngii*.

Many years ago I read a glowing description of the Black Birch, with striking peeling black bark, named *Betula nigra* in the text. Needless to say I succumbed to temptation and sent for a specimen. Today it is a most lovely small tree. I had feared it must be a hybrid as it has ragged cinnamon-coloured bark that I love to peel off whenever I feel in need of occupational therapy. Now the mystery is cleared up. The true Black Birch of America with the dark bark is *B. lenta* and *B. nigra* is the Red or River Birch and should have bark of a warm reddish-brown. The Swedish Birch, *B. p. dalecarlica*, was put in at the same time, but died. I do not think for one moment that this was the fault of the climate. Birch trees are quite hardy, coming as they do from northern climes, but on occasion they can be quite tricky to establish. I find the spring a better time to plant them than the autumn.

All the birches are wonderful in the wilder parts of the garden, and there are many more species and varieties from which to choose.

Probably the next most popular tree is the Mountain Ash or Rowan, *Sorbus aucuparia*, and nothing can be lovelier when it is bearing its crop of red fruits. Nor can the intense golden colour of its autumn foliage be surpassed by many other trees. Unfortunately the berries of the specimens in our garden are invariably eaten by the blackbirds before they are as much as ripe. I see rowans, laden with berries, growing in the heart of the countryside and the thought often crosses my mind: where have all the blackbirds gone? I am told that rhododendrons are allergic to *S. aucuparia*, or vice versa, and I should not be surprised, as the rhododendrons under some of our trees look far from happy.

Tempted by the catalogue description of *S. sargentiana*, I obtained a packet of seed. Only one germinated and I put it very carefully into what I thought was a good, sheltered position. Three years later it is still only about 6 inches tall, although, of course, I must agree with the catalogue description that it has large sticky buds!

Beeches, among the best loved of all English forest trees, are, unfortunately, too large for the average garden, but there is an upright form called *Fagus sylvatica fastigiata*, or the Dawyck Beech, named after the garden near Peebles in Scotland in which it originated. Beeches thrive on lime, but also grow quite well on neutral soils. The leaves are retained on the young trees throughout the winter months, giving the well-known russety effect.

The Purple Beech, *F. s. purpurea*, which I planted, has surprised me by its rate of growth, but it is not suitable for smaller gardens and indeed is, or will be eventually, far too large for my own. Nevertheless, the foliage looks well against the green of the other trees. There is, too, a more dainty beech, with fern-like leaves, named *F. s. laciniata*.

By the stream at the bottom of the garden we have a mature elm tree. Terrified by the thought that one day it might be blown down and that we should then be left with a gap, I planted a young horse chestnut in front of it. A subsequent gale proved the futility of the best laid schemes of mice and men by blowing the top off the young tree but mercifully leaving the elm alone. Fortunately our *Aesculus hippocastanum*, as the horse chestnut is called, has recovered, but I can only conclude that the wood of these trees is brittle, making them unsuitable subjects for planting in exposed positions. For anyone with a small garden, who likes the foliage of these plants, there is one of considerably less stature, the Red Buckeye, *A. pavia.*

Everyone likes the weeping willow, and if you have a fair-sized garden, with a stream at the foot, it is an obvious choice. The one I grow is *Salix alba tristis* (*S. vitellina pendula*). Each spring, long before it comes into leaf, one becomes aware, more and more each day, of the intensifying hue of its yellow buds, until at last each leaf emerges from its sheath on the cascading branches. Later on, the sound of cooing may come from a nest built on an inner platform and you know that it is being used as a nursery by the wood pigeons. In the autumn a large tawny owl may find protection in the canopy of its twigs and, with a mingled sense of satisfaction and relief, you realise that your garden has been accepted by nature as a sanctuary.

This willow, in common with most other members of its genus, is simple to propagate. Any piece torn off in the autumn, with a heel attached, and inserted to half its length in sandy soil, will have rooted by the following spring. These young plants may then be trained as standard trees by rubbing off a proportion of the lower buds each year until they reach a height of 8 to 10 feet, when the heads may then be allowed to develop. Do not rub off all the lower buds at once though, otherwise you will reduce the vigour of your plants. Remember, they breathe through their foliage.

There is another willow which 'pussies' so early in the year that people can hardly believe that it is real. This is the Violet Willow, *S. daphnoides*, named after the purplish-violet of its shoots.

I have recently fallen a victim to the charms of *S. fargesii.* I first saw this most striking shrub growing in the garden at Crathes Castle, near Banchory, in Scotland and have obtained a specimen, which I am hoping will be hardy here. Farge's Willow is a native of Central China. It is a rather spreading deciduous shrub reaching an eventual height of 6 to 8 feet, with shiny reddish-brown shoots and large glossy dark green leaves, a most effective contrast.

And now we come to the flowering trees, of which the best loved is the Golden Rain, or laburnum, in its two most popular forms *vossii* and *anagyroides*. The first of these is by far the better, having much longer racemes of flower. *L. vossii* is a hybrid of the Scotch Laburnum, *alpinum*, which blooms a little later and has, too, extremely long racemes. Believe it nor not, there was a laburnum in this garden when we first came here which was chopped down eventually because the buds got frost-nipped every spring and we never even saw a flower! All of these trees will survive the smokiest of town atmospheres and are extremely hardy, although they are not very long lived.

The next of the popular favourites must surely be the ornamental cherries. These grow well in the North and I find that bush specimens get away much more quickly than do standards.

In my youth I was lured by an article entitled 'Cherries from your Bedroom Window'. I visualised seeing the blossom while actually lying in bed. The idea had appeal. I planted my tree very close to the bedroom window and before many years had elapsed the cherry had an exceedingly good view of me in bed. Furthermore, it had darkened the whole of that side of the house, so had to come down. Can you guess which one it was? Yes, the deep pink, double *Prunus* Kanzan. A fine vigorous tree it well may be, but I got heartily sick of the particular colour combination of pink flowers and copper foliage and was quite pleased to see it go.

In the main the leaves of ornamental cherries seem as palatable to caterpillars as those of culinary fruit trees, so that unless you spray them, which I do not, the foliage presents a nasty tracery of holes during the summer months. It is as well, therefore, to plant specimens away from the immediate vicinity of the house, unless you wish to be constantly reminded of your shortcomings.

My own special favourite among the ornamental cherries is the species *P. yedoensis* or Yoshino. If you can bear to wait several years, you will be rewarded by a lovely graceful tree, the first to bloom among those growing here. The blossom opens on the bare twigs but before the single white flowers unfold their delicately perfumed petals, *P. yedoensis* is quite entrancing in the pattern of its pinkish buds. Seen against a back-ground of blue sky it is incredibly beautiful. Of late years the bull-finches have played havoc with the precocious buds but, as gardeners, we hope that they will have a go at something fresh next year, or leave the district. Actually there is now a bird deterrent spray on the market which I intend to use.

A few years ago, to my delight, my two trees bore a few small black cherries, which I planted in a pot and promptly forgot. Imagine my surprise when, in the following spring, nine sturdy seedlings showed themselves. These were put in a nursery bed where they were chewed down by rabbits the following winter. After this natural pruning they made well-shaped little bushes and I am hoping to see them in flower within the next few years. Meantime I am enjoying the magnificent colour of their autumn foliage.

There are two standard Sargent's Cherries, *P. sargentii*, growing in the copse, where they have been for over 20 years. I bought them in the first place for the glorious autumn tints they were said to assume. I have seen other specimens shimmering in their translucent cornelian dress and have been impressed by their quite obvious splendour, but mine, so far, have only given indifferent displays of fleeting character. The pale pink single flowers of this species open with, and are often almost hidden by, the unfolding leaves. The autumn-flowering cherry, *P. subhirtella autumnalis*, is, on the other hand, spreading, dainty and out to please. It makes noble attempts to flower at the first sign of a mild spell in both autumn and winter, but this is an inclement spot and I am always relieved to see that the bulk of the flower buds have the good sense to wait until the spring before opening.

There is in my garden, too, a Weeping Spring Cherry, *P. s. pendula*, but it has not done as well as my neighbour's half-standard, and cannot match the superb pair of these trees growing in one of the famous Irish gardens. As in the case of the *P. sargentii*, it is a standard specimen.

These small-flowered cherries are so dainty, either in or out of flower, that they are cherished favourites, so much so that I have recently planted another one by the name of Pandora. This is growing apace and has already released from her 'box' not only an attractive spring display of pale pink single flowers, but a marvellous autumn dress of amber and gold.

The Oshima cherry, *P. serrulata albida*, was sent to me as a substitute and, so far, I am not particularly impressed. It has rather too stiff a habit for my taste. The single flowers are white, bearing a strong fragrance, but as they open at the same time as the leaves unfold, they seem to get somewhat lost.

Another substitute for the lovely Gean, *P. avium flore pleno*, came in the shape of *P. cerasus rhexii*. By my standards the flowers of this hybrid were too tight and the growth too cramped, but the wood burned well when the trees were felled!

A mature specimen of that double pale pink beauty Hokusai (*P. serrulata spiralis*) that I saw growing in a garden on the outskirts of our local town induced me to acquire one of my own. It is of typical Japanese form and is growing well, even although it is planted in rough grass.

We are told to keep the roots of newly planted trees and shrubs clear

Steps lead up to a small lawn in the author's garden; *Malus spectabilis* marks the change of level

The Fishbone Cotoneaster, *Cotoneaster horizontalis*, makes excellent cover for walls and banks

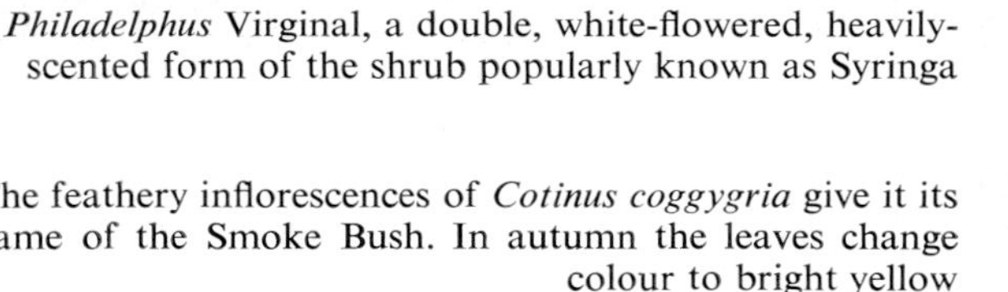

Philadelphus Virginal, a double, white-flowered, heavily-scented form of the shrub popularly known as Syringa

The feathery inflorescences of *Cotinus coggygria* give it its name of the Smoke Bush. In autumn the leaves change colour to bright yellow

of grass for at least five years, and this is excellent advice. The difference in growth between specimens growing in the open ground and in rough grass has to be seen to be appreciated; and if you wish to give your plants the best possible start in life, I can only advise you to do as the experts say in this respect.

The most Japanese-looking of my cherries is Mount Fuji (*P.* Shirotae), a large-leaved, sprawling tree, somewhat frost-tender and therefore not too reliable for a regular spring display in a low-lying garden. Nevertheless, the flowers are enormous and it is the first choice as far as I am concerned for an early white Japanese variety.

Another white-flowered cherry, Tai-haku, planted later than the Mount Fuji, has not yet reached the size where it may be fairly judged, but it is growing quite well. The flowers open at the same time as the copper foliage and I am not at all sure that I like this combination of colour. When this tree came to me I was puzzled by a silver sheen on the leaves. On reflection I realised that this was a slight case of Silver Leaf. I consulted my text books and found that the cure was to remove the offending branches, in this case the whole of the tree. Then I remembered someone else's advice, which was 'to let the devil out of the bark'. The trick was to cut the main stem on the north side vertically from tip to toe. With some scepticism and a cynical laugh at the 'devil', I did this and, to my amazement, there has not been a trace of Silver Leaf since. It was certainly not a case of faith healing!

Two wonderful later-flowering double white cherries are *P. s. longipes* (Shimidsu Sakura) and *P. s. albo-rosea* (Shirofugen). The latter, a recent favourite, grew a Witch's Broom, which, for those who may not have heard of this term, is the common name of a fungus disease. Growth stood still until this was removed, since when the tree has formed a graceful spreading head. Here again, the foliage is coppery but the flowers open with a pinkish flush and the colour association is just right. *P. s. longipes* has green leaves, but to stand underneath either of these trees when they are in flower, and look up into the branches, is a delight.

Bullfinches leave the buds of the late-flowering cherries alone; there is better hunting at that period in the fruit orchard. A reliable display is assured, even in the frostiest of gardens.

A pair of space-saving 'Lombardy Poplar' cherries, *P. s. erecta* or Amanogawa, flank a yew enclosure, but these no longer appeal to me, in spite of the pale pink blossom having the delightful scent of almonds. Stiffness in plants, as in people, means to me a distinct loss of charm. Then, too, these trees are apt to become sprawly with age unless care is taken to prune and train them correctly in the early stages.

A less flamboyant double pink than Kanzan, flowering slightly later and not so stiff in growth, is *P. s.* Fugenzo. I prefer this one of the two, but it is altogether a matter of personal choice.

I get a number of local enquiries about the Bird Cherry, *P. padus watereri*. This tree does well in my garden growing in rough grass and so neglected that I omitted to cut out a parallel stem which it grew when my back was turned. The double head has now grown into a well-shaped specimen, making a beautiful picture in spring. The Bird Cherry does not seem to be well enough known and the creamy-white plumes of tiny flowers appear to dissociate it in the mind of the layman from the prunus family.

Almonds, *P. amygdalus*, are not really satisfactory in my district. They certainly stay alive but grow poorly, sucker badly and there is a fair amount of die-back annually. This may be partly due to the lack of lime in the soil as there is a good specimen growing a few miles away.

In my early gardening days I tried the Chinese Peach, *P. davidiana*, also the double peach, *P. persica* Clara Meyer. The first died on me without even opening its eyes and the last got itself turfed out as that, too, was diminishing in size every time I looked at it. Really, unless there is a sunny sheltered position against a wall to be offered to these lovers of warmer climes, it is better to exclude them from the garden altogether and spend your money on something of which you can be reasonably certain.

Among the most popular spring-flowering trees are the Flowering Crabs, species and varieties of *Malus*. The difficult point to decide in selecting these sweetly scented, dome-shaped, small trees is whether to have the ones with the green leaves, or the ones with the purple ones. Now those with the purple foliage, to me, give the finer spring effects, as, before unfolding, the leaf buds are bright red. When the pink flowers are out the leaves are bronzy-red, giving a fine colour contrast. Among these are *M. purpurea*, *M. lemoinei* and *M. eleyi*. On the debit side, the foliage of these darken with age to a most uninteresting dull purplish colour, giving the trees a drab look until leaf-fall.

Of the green-leaved species, the Japanese Crab, *M. floribunda*, and the Chinese *M. spectabilis* are extremely dainty, both producing an amazing profusion of blush-coloured flowers that contrast well with the crimson buds.

One of my favourites is *M. sargentii.* This grows to a height of about 8 feet and, in the spring, is literally smothered with masses of white flowers, each with conspicuous golden anthers. It is quite liberal in the provision of self-sown seedlings from the small red berries, with which it adorns itself in the autumn.

Of the fruiting crabs, the most widely planted variety is John Downie. Beautiful as this is when covered with its brightly coloured oblong fruits, may I also put in a plea for the very fine Veitch's Scarlet? Here, the more cylindrically shaped fruits are about twice the size of John Downie and, of course, both kinds are in demand for the making of crab apple jelly. If you have some fruits of *eleyi* or *purpurea*, the inclusion of a few fruits of these varieties will improve the colour of the jelly.

The crabs I have mentioned are all quite hardy, although you may find that you have to protect the stems of young specimens if you live in rabbit country. The best way to do this is to wrap wire netting round the base. The height of the netting will depend how much snow you expect to get in the winter months in your district. When the snow is on the ground the rabbits are extremely voracious and I have known them nibble the bark of trees 4 feet from the ground.

As with the cherries, I prefer to grow crabs in bush form as they will then form large dome shapes, well furnished to the ground. Grown as standards, they take longer to mature and then form trees with mop-shaped heads.

While most of the ornamental cherries will produce spectacular autumn tints, ranging from clear yellows through shades of orange and red, I find the crabs unsatisfying in this respect.

The Snowy Mespilus or June Berry, *Amelanchier canadensis*, is another small tree which I thought I would try after reading an enthusiastic report as to its merits. It has short, buddleia-like racemes of white flowers, looser and shorter, but rather similar in appearance to those of the Bird Cherry. The autumn tints, for which it is most lauded, have been disappointing and exceedingly fleeting. Among all the small trees growing here, this is usually the first to lose its leaves, and I am sure that it would have gone to the bonfire many years ago had it not been in a neglected corner of the garden.

Halesia carolina, the Snowdrop Tree, captured my imagination, I rather suspect, because I used to belong to the Snowdrop Patrol in the

Girl Guides. It got frost-nipped regularly, so I gave it to one of my local friends gardening in a slightly more elevated position. It has not fared much better there either, so that I conclude that our climate is, once again, too cold.

I grow only one magnolia. When choosing magnolias in the first place I read so much about them that I was too intimidated to try any but the hardiest, *Magnolia liliflora nigra.* My *Magnolia liliflora nigra* has grown into a bush about 6 feet high and as much through. It bears a wonderful crop of the most beautiful goblet-shaped blooms, rosy-purple outside and paler within. Sometimes a proportion of these are caught by the frost, but it flowers successionally and there are always some buds to come. When untouched by the late spring frosts it is a lovely bush and I am grateful for the pleasure it gives me for so many weeks of the year. It likes a peaty loam and, topdressed with peat, the lower branches layer easily, the large fleshy white roots greedily thrusting themselves into the more friable medium. This magnolia is growing open to the full force of the westerly winds and has assumed a sturdy ground-hugging habit. As the wood has the reputation of being brittle, it has found the perfect method of avoiding damage. Not a branch has been broken off by the wind all the time it has been here. It is recommended that magnolias are planted in April when they are moving into growth.

Of course, if I were beginning all over again I should be tempted to try some of the white-flowered magnolias, which I much prefer. The popular *M. stellata*, a specimen of which is growing in a local garden, does not seem too successful in this neighbourhood. Perhaps I should choose the magnificent *M. wilsonii*, with pendent, strongly perfumed flowers. There is one of this type thriving a few miles away, in a less polluted district, that gives me encouragement.

I have almost forgotten to mention one of my favourite trees, a deciduous conifer, the Common Larch, *Larix decidua.* No other tree can exceed the beauty of its soft green spring foliage. Recently I have planted several specimens of the Japanese Larch, *L. leptolepis*, and these seem to be growing more quickly than the common larch.

There is one tree that I would like readers to avoid planting, although it is one of the best ones for silver foliage effects. This is the White Poplar, or *Populus alba*, and was given to us when we first started the garden to help fill in. It has the lethal habit of surface rooting, suckering for yards and yards, so that life becomes a perpetual struggle between gardener and poplar. Its suckers appear right in the middle of the choicest plants, a terrific heave bringing up plants, bulbs and seemingly miles of the wretched tree root which, if left untraced to source, starts its tricks all over again a little further on.

And this brings me to the warning I want to issue to anyone who is at the outset of his or her gardening life. Kind friends, and I use the word 'kind' without any trace of implied denigration, are apt to give away a lot of rubbish to start you off that may end up by putting you off for life. An example of this is the Snow-in-Summer, or *Cerastium tomentosum.* I have seen this plant looking most effective outside gardens, with its silver foliage falling over a wall, but this is where it belongs—outside the garden. It is a relative of the native chickweed, and just as tiresome. Do not have it in the garden. Other favourite discards are Golden Rod (*Solidago*) and Michaelmas daisies in their most miserable forms. Here again, in their better varieties they are most welcome, but they both seed themselves with such freedom that much dross finds its way into the gold.

I wonder whether I might appeal to gardeners to grow more trees from seed? Such plants are usually much better doers than grafted or budded specimens, and think of the range of choice open to you. When I waft my watering-can over my seed pans, I feel like the dictator to end all dictators. What shall I grow? Shall it be the flamboyant marigold, the magical poppy from Tibet, or the Cedar of Lebanon? I am the one to conjure up these things from their sleep, as the Fairy Prince kissed the Princess into life. There is more romance in a packet of seeds than a whole library of love stories.

PLANTS REFERRED TO IN THIS CHAPTER

Name	*Origin of species*	*Ultimate height*	*Description*	*Annual rate of growth in author's garden*
Aesculus hippocastanum	N. Greece, Albania	100ft.	White flowers in June followed by 'conkers'.	12in.
pavia	Southern U.S.A.	8–12ft.	Crimson flowers in June.	
Amelanchier canadensis	E. and Central N. America	20–30ft.	White flowers. Good autumn tints.	6–9in.
Betula lenta	N. America	50–60ft.	Black peeling bark.	
nigra	Eastern U.S.A.	50–60ft.	Reddish-brown bark.	9–12in.
pendula	Europe	50–60ft.	Lovely in the wilder parts of the garden.	9–12in.

Name	*Origin of species*	*Ultimate height*	*Description*	*Annual rate of growth in author's garden*
Betula pendula				
dalecarlica		50–60ft.	Elegant deeply cut foliage.	
youngii		20–30ft.	Graceful small weeping tree, ultimately with dome-shaped head.	15ft. after 20 years.
Cornus alba	Siberia	8ft.	The Red-barked Dogwood, very effective in winter.	3ft.
sibirica		8ft.	The Westonbirt Dogwood, Bark bright crimson.	
Fagus sylvatica fastigiata		40–50ft.	Upright form, for economy of space. The Dawyck Beech.	
laciniata		Up to 80ft.	The Fern-leaved Beech. Magnificent in its ultimate perfection.	
purpurea		Up to 100ft.	The Purple Beech.	12in.
Halesia carolina	Southern U.S.A.	20–25ft.	The Snowdrop Tree. White flowers in May on pendulous stalks.	
Laburnum				
alpinum	Central and S. Europe	20ft.	Long racemes of yellow flowers. So well known that we are apt to lose sight of the fact that it is one of the most beautiful of flowering trees. June.	6–12in.
anagyroides	,,	20ft.	The Common Laburnum, Golden Chain.	6–12in.
vossii		20ft.	Just as impressive as *alpinum*.	6–12in.
Larix				
decidua	N. and Central Europe	Up to 100ft.	Soft green foliage in the spring. A lovely tree.	12in.
leptolepis	Japan	Up to 80ft.	Grows more rapidly than *decidua* in this area.	18–24in.
Magnolia liliflora nigra		12ft.	Goblet-shaped flowers, rosy-purple outside, paler within. The best for a frost hole. May/June.	6–12in.
stellata	Japan	10ft.	White flowers in April. The best species for a small garden.	

Name	*Origin of species*	*Ultimate height*	*Description*	*Annual rate of growth in author's garden*
Magnolia wilsonii	Szechwan	Up to 25ft.	Pendent, strongly perfumed flowers in May/June.	
Malus eleyi		Up to 25ft.	Pink flowers April/May, dome-shaped tree with purplish foliage.	12–18in.
floribunda	Japan	Up to 20ft.	Round-headed tree, flowers rosy-red in bud, pink on opening. Green foliage.	12–18in.
John Downie		20–30ft.	Grown for its brightly coloured oblong fruits.	
lemoinei		Up to 25ft.	Pink flowers in April/May, bronzy-red leaves, leaf buds bright red before unfolding.	12–18in.
purpurea		Up to 25ft.	Flowers ruby-red in bud, more purplish when open.	12–18in.
sargentii	Japan	10–12ft.	White flowers with golden anthers in spring. Small red berries in autumn. Seeds itself freely.	12in.
spectabilis	N. China	30ft.	Tree of rounded habit. Green leaves, flowers rosy-red in bud, blush-tinted when open. A glorious sight in May.	12in.
Veitch's Scarlet		20–30ft.	Scarlet, rounded crab apples. A glorious sight in the autumn.	12in.
Prunus avium flore pleno		60ft.	One of the most beautiful of flowering trees. White blossom in April/May.	
cerasus rhexii		20ft.	Tight white flowers in spring.	
padus watereri		20–40ft.	The Bird Cherry. Flowers in racemes, creamy-white. Spring.	12in.
sargentii	Japan	30–35ft.	Pale pink flowers in early spring, wonderful autumn colour.	9–12in.

Name	*Origin of species*	*Ultimate height*	*Description*	*Annual rate of growth in author's garden*
Prunus				
serrulata				
albida		20–30ft.	Single white flowers, strong fragrance.	12in.
albo rosea (Shirofugen)		25–30ft.	Late-flowering double white.	12in.
erecta (Amanogawa)		20ft.	Fragrant pale pink flowers mid-season. Lombardy poplar habit.	12in.
Fugenzo		20–25ft.	Double pink, late flowering.	12in.
Kanzan		25–30ft.	Double, pink flowers, young foliage copper. Very vigorous.	12–24in.
longipes (Shimidsu Sakura)		15ft.	Green foliage, white flowers. A late variety.	6–12in.
Shirotae (Mount Fuji)		15ft.	Sprawling, early, white-flowered tree.	18–24in.
spiralis (Hokusai)		30ft.	Vigorous growth but apt to suffer from dieback. Semi-double pale pink. Mid-season.	6in. in rough grass.
Tai-haku		25–30ft.	Mid-season, white flowers and copper foliage.	12–15in.
subhirtella				
autumnalis		30ft.	Spreading, dainty habit. Pinkish-white flowers. October/April.	12in.
Pandora		20ft.	Branches wreathed with single pink flowers in early spring. Good autumn tints.	12–15in.
pendula		15–30ft.	Branches wreathed with single pink flowers in early spring.	6–9in.
yedoensis (Yoshino)	Japan	30ft.	Early flowering before the leaves. Graceful arching growth. Beware bullfinches.	12–18in.
Salix alba tristis (*S. vitellina pendula*)		65ft.	The Weeping Willow. Yellow buds in spring.	2–3ft.
daphnoides	Europe, Asia	30ft.	Purplish-violet shoots. Catkins in spring.	12in.

Name	*Origin of species*	*Ultimate height*	*Description*	*Annual rate of growth in author's garden*
Salix				
fargesii	Central China	6–8ft.	Glossy dark green leaves. Brightly coloured winter buds and catkins in spring.	3–6in.
Sorbus				
aucuparia	Europe and Asia	30–60ft.	The Mountain Ash. Red fruits and golden autumn foliage. Grows nearly anywhere and seeds itself freely.	12–18in.
sargentiana	Western China	20–30ft.	Pinnate leaves 8–12in. long. White flowers in May, scarlet fruits. Too slow from seed. Buy a specimen, at least if you live in the West Riding of Yorkshire!	2–3in.

CHAPTER THREE

Good-tempered Shrubs

Life's dearest mysteries lie near, not far,
The least explored are the familiar, ...

W. de la Mare

It is the most difficult thing in the world to garden from scratch in an urban area and make an immediate effect, without using annuals, perennials, or rose trees. I am sure that is the reason why so many privet hedges are planted. At least they provide the garden with body in its initial stages.

When I am trying to think of a flowering shrub almost as accommodating as privet, I immediately think of the common broom, *Cytisus scoparius*. This tolerant plant grows very quickly and a packet of mixed seeds will provide all kinds of colour variations and in three or four years you will have some sizeable shrubs. It will probably be safer to grow them in pots until you have decided upon the permanent positions, as brooms dislike being moved. To keep them in good shape the young plants should be clipped over in the spring, never cutting into the old wood, but clipping sufficiently to keep them symmetrical. They will provide an immediate effect while the slower growing shrubs are establishing themselves, when they may be cut down if desired.

The nicest of the hybrid brooms to my mind is *C. praecox*, one of the first to flower, and a foam of creamy blossom. It has one drawback in that it has rather an unpleasant perfume. Seedlings of this species do not come true but they are often similar in colour to the parent plant.

The White Broom, *C. albus*, is a favourite with many people but it is short-lived with me and seems to have a weaker constitution than many of the coloured varieties.

The Spanish Broom, *Spartium junceum*, has a different habit altogether. This one flowers later in the summer, is golden-yellow in colour and has a most delicious fragrance. It has rather rush-like foliage and becomes extremely straggly unless it is clipped back each year. Most years it seeds itself freely, which is a good thing as it, too, like most of this family, is short-lived.

For that gayest of spring-flowering shrubs, the forsythia, I have nothing but praise, and where would those who have to garden in towns be without it? For the disposition of the flowers along the stem, my first choice must be *Forsythia suspensa*. How graceful it looks cascading over a wall, and how hardy these forsythias are, never failing to grow in the most unpromising soil and keeping the proud owners constantly stocked with self-layered young plants. Some people complain to me that their bushes do not flower well, but I think this is often due to the fact that they are planted against a wall where there is no sun, consequently the wood does not ripen.

There is a large specimen of *F. suspensa fortunei* here. Other than for filling up the garden I would not recommend this variety, for during the 25 years of its life I do not think it has given even one reasonable display of flowers, and it is growing in the open!

Forsythia intermedia spectabilis, on the other hand, never fails to cover itself with richly coloured blooms every year. *F. viridissima* flowers slightly later than *spectabilis* and if you have room for only one bush, do not choose this species as there are much nicer varieties.

I have recently planted a specimen of *F.* Beatrix Farrand but it is too early for me to pass judgment yet. It certainly has extra large deep yellow flowers. As I have read so much about *F.* Lynwood it, also, has been added to my collection. This is reputed to be the finest of all the Golden Bell bushes but here again I have not had it long enough to be able to pass an opinion.

We are told to prune these shrubs immediately after flowering as they flower on the new wood. Not with me. Only the old wood bears flower buds, so I prune forsythias solely to shape them and to remove dead and unwanted wood. I find that forsythias are easily propagated by cuttings. Young shoots about 3 inches long, taken off the bushes in the spring, root readily in pots of moist sandy loam.

Really I do not know why I bother with forsythias at all, on account of the influx of bullfinches into the garden during the last few years. But I make sure of having some flowers by bringing a few branches from my shrubs into the house early in the New Year. Sparrows can be most destructive too, and I suppose I subconsciously think that if I have a large enough number of bushes there will be more flower buds than they can find time to destroy. Still, it is all most maddening.

The Flowering Currant, *Ribes sanguineum*, is among the most popular of the 'easy' shrubs, as it can literally put up with almost any soil and position. There are some good forms of it and if you would like a nice bright red, you should choose either Pulborough Scarlet or *splendens*. Another crimson variety, dwarfer than the type, is King Edward VII.

The wishy-washy *R. sanguineum albidum* is, to me, a doubtful choice. So reasonably priced are these shrubs, however, that I have recently planted a specimen of this variety to see whether it is quite as dowdy as it looks in other people's gardens, or whether it has some hidden charms that I have overlooked, such as suitability for floral arrangements and so on. If it has been misjudged then I shall keep it, if not, out it will go. All these forms have a rather spicy fragrance which appeals to me. Other people find the scent most unpleasant.

A friend gave me a cutting of *R. odoratum* many years ago. She had been growing it successfully in industrial Lancashire, where I had admired the yellow, clove-scented flowers. She has since moved to the drier east Yorkshire coast and it has been an utter failure there. This is interesting. I kept my cutting of this ribes that she had given me for 15 years, during which time it grew no more than 2 feet high and rarely bore a flower. When she told me what had happened to her plant in its new surroundings, I felt justified in booting mine out.

I should like to be able to grow *R. speciosum*. This is a Californian shrub with dark red flowers, rather like fuchsias, but so far I have not dared to try it.

In spite of their thorns, I must mention one or two of the deciduous barberries, so valuable are they for autumn effects and berries. *Berberis thunbergii* is outstanding for autumn colour and its variety *atropurpurea* provides a good foliage plant of rich reddish-purple. I saw this shrub clipped to shape being used extensively for colour effect on rock gardens in Germany, and as a foil for some of the more glaring orange floribunda roses. I have just planted a couple of specimens of an even smaller form, *B. t. atropurpurea nana*. This should be ideal for a small rock garden. *B. wilsonae* quite outshines the *thunbergii* varieties in the production of the most wonderful coral berries. Picked for house decoration, these are terrific and never fail to excite admiration.

The genus *Cotoneaster* is one which I find especially useful. The Fishbone Cotoneaster, *C. horizontalis*, is a little shrub which is indispensable in one or another part of the garden. It will clothe a bank, climb a wall, or cover a manhole. Bees love the flowers and the birds love its berries. One of the prettiest sights I have seen in connection with this cotoneaster, was a shy mother wren, with her family of five, seeking spiders in its branches. One of my friends, living near the east coast, was lucky enough to see a flock of that rare bird of passage, the waxwing, dining on the berries of a specimen of this cotoneaster growing outside one of her windows. There is a variegated form of it, *C. h. variegatus,* that is even more charming, but in spite of having tried it once or twice, I cannot persuade it to stay with me. On reflection I realise that I have lost quite a number of cotoneasters of one kind and another during the course of my gardening career, and consider that it might be a better idea for the nurseryman to sell all of them in pots, as I am sure that once the roots become dry, in many cases the plants die.

Cotoneaster microphyllus has smaller, evergreen leaves and is quite hardy. This also is an excellent plant for covering walls and in its form *C. m. thymifolius* is a perfect rock shrub.

I bought a *C. adpressus* two years ago and am delighted with its habit. It has leaves larger than *C. horizontalis*, enormous red berries and more arching branches. The edges of the leaves are slightly wavy, and I am wondering whether this is not, in fact, the more vigorous form *adpressus praecox*, known in gardens as Nan-shan. Whatever it is, it is a decided acquisition, being extremely vigorous and already putting forth roots on the more prostrate of its branches. *Cotoneaster frigidus* is a most attractive semi-evergreen. It grows into quite a large bush, or small tree, and is of pleasing form. I should think that it would berry more freely in a less frosty garden than this, but the attraction to me lies in the fresh green colour of its leaves and the way in which they are arranged along its branches.

There is such a host of cotoneasters that it would be quite impossible to include all of them in any but the largest of gardens. *C. salicifolius*, the Willow-leaved cotoneaster, is, in its variety *floccosus*, particularly graceful, and the branches when cut are ideal for decorative effect.

Many of these shrubs are described as evergreen in the catalogues, but that is not true in this part of the country where in the winter, more often than not, they lose the better part of their leaves. Cotoneasters will tolerate nearly any conditions but to me they have one failing. They are prone to a rather peculiar fungoid disease which makes the stems die back and spoils the symmetry of the growth.

Everyone knows the common lilac, *Syringa vulgaris*. It grows practically everywhere, so there is no need for me to say much about it.

Lilacs do best on a soil that has a proportion of lime in its content. They are heavy feeders and appreciate a rich diet. Most people admire the double white, *S.* Madame Lemoine, and the single dark red variety, *S.* Souvenir de Louis Späth, is a favourite of mine. Katherine Havemeyer is another lovely variety, but I am sure that if you like one lilac you will like them all and it is better that you should make your own choice, either from a nursery or botanical garden, where you will be able to look at some of the species as well.

The shrub which many people call Syringa is actually the philadelphus. In my opinion, the best double white one is the variety Virginal, that gorgeously perfumed plant bearing its heavy crop of blossom in June when the first flush of spring-flowering shrubs is over. If you like the smaller kinds, then Belle Etoile is delightful, the large single flowers being flushed in the centre with maroon. These are not as fragrant as those of Virginal.

Last year, for the first time, I saw a magnificent specimen of a variegated philadelphus called Innocence. I am sure this is not as well known as it should be and, as I thought it most effective, I am going to try one in my own garden. Also new to me was *P. coronarius aureus* which looked extremely attractive in its spring dress of bright yellow.

Philadelphus microphyllus is a dainty small-leaved species of compact habit, forming a bush of about 3 feet. It is a native of such parts of North America as Colorado and Arizona, and although it comes from such a hot, sunny climate, I think I shall try it against my west wall, as it is said to succeed remarkably well in the British Isles.

In spite of the blameless names of some of these Orange Blossoms, they get very untidy if left to their own devices and should be cut back occasionally to keep them within bounds. The best time to do this is immediately they have finished flowering. I propagate philadelphus from softwood cuttings of the same length as advised in the case of the forsythias. The time to take them can be judged by the colour of the base of the shoot, which should have turned a pale tan.

The weigelas (diervillas) are not particular favourites of mine, but the hybrids are almost indestructible. Having purchased one many years ago for what, in those days, was the remarkable sum of sixpence, I crammed it into an unprepared hole at the foot of a wall facing due east. The morning sun shone upon it for probably two hours each day, normal light being further obstructed by a building projection. Notwithstanding this treatment, the weigela grew and prospered and rewarded my churlishness by covering itself with a mass of pale pink flowers year after year, until finally it had to be dug up to make way for an extension to the house. There are varying colours of hybrid weigelas from cream to deep red and they are to be recommended for difficult sites.

There is one weigela which I consider to be among the best of variegated shrubs. This is *W. florida variegata*, and it does not appear to be as straggling, nor as vigorous as the other hybrids. It has pretty pale pink flowers and softwood cuttings root readily.

If you like purple-foliaged plants, there is a purple weigela which goes by the name of *W. f. foliis purpureis*, but personally I find this rather a dull shrub. There is also a yellow-flowered species named *W. middendorffiana*, but this is less hardy, preferring a milder climate.

The Japanese Quince, or chaenomeles, is a favourite shrub for growing against house walls. Its apple-blossom-like flowers appear in early spring, and the most popular form is scarlet. It prefers lime in the soil which is possibly why it does not do very well in my garden. The Japanese Quince is supposed to have been the forbidden fruit in the Garden of Eden, an irrelevant but interesting snippet of information which I bring to your notice.

Short of a miracle, once you plant a chaenomeles, it is with you for life. In the right conditions it is a most beautiful shrub and when I see it in other gardens I am always full of enthusiasm. I acquired my first plant from our sixpenny store. I feel sure that it must have been the species *Chaenomeles japonica* as it has grown no more than a couple of feet high, each spring producing a few sporadic orange-red flowers. These, in turn, have been followed by a few yellow quinces, so if you are gardening in this or a similar area, I would advise you to skip this one and concentrate on the *C. speciosa* hybrids. Of these, Rowallane Seedling is a fine variety, having scarlet-crimson flowers with petals of thick texture. It is almost identical to *C.* x *superba* Knap Hill Scarlet. There are other named hybrids, for instance *rosea flore pleno*, double rose-pink; *nivalis*, white; and *moerloesii*, pink and white.

Of the early-flowering shrubs the Mezereon, *Daphne mezereum*, is among the most widely planted. There are varying shades of reddish-mauve flowers, the darker being preferable. It has a superb perfume, is perfectly hardy, but has the annoying habit of deciding suddenly that it does not like your face. This daphne may flower well for years and just as you are congratulating yourself upon having a good specimen, it dies.

On the credit side, it berries well and a few seedling plants can usually be found at its foot once it has started to flower regularly, always provided, of course, that the birds do not eat the berries before they have time to germinate. If you find any seedlings, pot them up carefully until you are sure where you want to place them, as this is one of the shrubs which hates being moved, and moving a bush is the surest way of killing it. There is a white-flowered form of this, *D. m. alba*, but my personal preference is for the pink. The Mezereon is often said to be winter-flowering, but in my garden it is rarely in bloom before the end of March.

I keep thinking that perhaps I should try to grow some other members of the daphne family, chiefly on account of their delightful perfume, but they are such temperamental plants that I prefer others to have the trouble of them.

Every gardener should be persuaded to try a *Spiraea arguta*. Dainty, foolproof and perfect for cutting, this is a lady's shrub, with all the refinement of the thoroughbred. The tiny snow-white flowers appear on bare twigs and the person who has not seen an arrangement of the Foam of May with white narcissi has missed one of the pleasures of spring. It will grow without attention for years, eventually reaching a height of about 6 feet, until one day you may realise that it has outgrown its position. Then you may prune it right down to the ground and it will shoot from the bottom again. After many unsuccessful attempts to propagate this plant, I have reached the conclusion that the easiest way to increase it is to divide it. The leaves colour to shades of yellow and orange before falling in the autumn.

Spiraea thunbergii is another small shrub, of less height ultimately than *S. arguta* and rather unlike it in that the flowers appear at the same time as the leaves. In this it is not nearly so attractive, although it has dainty green foliage that I used to cut when I wanted some greenery for floral arrangements. As my specimen of *S. thunbergii* was planted in a wind-swept position where it never looked its best, eventually I got rid of it.

I am not at all keen on *S. japonica alba*, nor yet on its cousin *S. bumalda* Anthony Waterer. These varieties do not seem to be happy in this soil, but I have seen plants that I have admired growing elsewhere.

I am sneaking in a shrub here which is not in my own garden but which is growing very well locally. This is *Rubus deliciosus*, a thornless bramble which hails from the Rocky Mountains. In May the arching branches are wreathed with snow-white flowers, rather like dog roses,

Cornus canadensis is the Creeping Dogwood, with creamy-white flowers in summer and bright red berries in the autumn

Hydrangeas are handsome plants and Générale Vicomtesse de Vibraye (a blue variety on acid soils, pink on alkaline soils unless these are treated), grows extremely well in the author's garden

The tiers of white flowers of the Lanarth Variety of *Viburnum tomentosum* are produced in May and June

Rhododendron praecox is a small hybrid growing to about 3 to 4 feet. The rosy-purple flowers appear in April-May

and if you would like to grow an uncommon shrub, then this is the one to choose. *R.* Tridel is a slightly more expensive and more up-to-date hybrid. What I like about these brambles is that they have no thorns and do not run about. What I dislike about them is the difficulty of propagation. I have made several attempts at rooting cuttings taken from my neighbour's bush in July. They are not easy. Just recently, having first treated them with hormone powder, I put some cuttings in a sand-filled pot, which I then covered with polythene. After a few weeks two of them looked fine, so I removed the polythene to give them some air. Too soon! They immediately had a relapse and I must now wait another year before trying again.

When people come round the garden in high summer, the interested ones always pause in front of my bush of *Cotinus coggygria foliis purpureis* Notcutt's Variety. This is no surprise to me as I have been a devotee of this particular one-time member of the rhus family for many years.

I was a complete stranger to gardening before my marriage. Until then I had either lived in towns or in places where fruit growing was the primary consideration. So, when I had a garden of my own, hours of my time in the winter evenings were devoted to thumbing through fat catalogues and reading whatever books on gardening I could lay my hands upon.

There was a large *Rhus typhina*, or Stag's-horn Sumach, growing in a local garden, but the owner did not know what it was. It is an easy plant to identify as the stems are covered with soft silky fur, rather like that on a stag's antlers. It is also sometimes known as the Walking Stick Plant, due to its habit of throwing suckers some distance from the parent plant.

Let me digress here, because this neighbour, who has long since died, was a character. His views on people were roughly those of mine on plants, and I remember his telling me what I considered to be a rather funny story. This man just hated people to stand at the door talking, saying that they would not come in as they were not stopping. One day a particularly tiresome lady had been dithering about on his step, neither coming nor going, as you might say. It was a bitterly cold day and our friend's chair was opposite the door, through which an icy blast was blowing. In exasperation, having asked her to come in for the tenth time, he snarled: 'If tha's coomin' in, coom in, and if tha's going 'ome, —— off.'

Having tracked down the name rhus in the catalogues and deciding, from the description, that my neighbour possessed a Stag's-horn Sumach, for which I had formed the greatest admiration, I pursued my investigations into the family and decided that, as described by the experts, *Rhus cotinus* (or *Cotinus coggygria,* as it is now known), the Smoke Bush, sounded most attractive. As we were in the process of making a shrubbery, an order was promptly despatched for one *Cotinus coggygria* and one *C. c. foliis purpureis.* These duly arrived as small specimens of about 1 foot in height and were planted with due ceremony. As they were just 'leaves' I cannot say I was over-impressed by them until about 12 years later when, all of a sudden, I realised that they were grown up. There again, you will probably think them just ordinary foliage shrubs until they reach a height of about 3 feet when it will possibly occur to you, as it did to me, that the experts are sometimes right.

It had never occurred to me either that most of our garden plants are growing wild in the world somewhere or other and no one could have been more astonished than I when I saw lavender and *C. coggygria* growing on the French Alps. It seemed to me that immediate steps should be taken to fence them in.

But to revert to Notcutt's Variety. This is a most striking purple-foliaged shrub with spoon-shaped leaves. Like others of its kind, in the spring it is rather a late starter, but it makes up for this by intensifying its hue during the whole of the summer until, in late October, its leaves fall in a final blaze of orange-crimson glory. I have found all the *C. coggygria* hybrids to be of slow growth, but they easily layer down if encouraged to do so with the help of a little sandy soil placed over the lower branches and secured by a stone.

Cotinus Notcutt's Variety looks even more striking when surrounded by plants with grey foliage and there are masses of the Lavender Cotton, *Santolina chamaecyparissus,* planted round my specimen. If you can give it a position where the sun can strike through the leaves, you will like it even more. A friend suggested that blue flowers would form a pleasing association with it too, so I am thinking of planting some varieties of *Aster amellus* nearby.

I have found also that these *C. coggygria* bushes are slow to flower, that is, to produce their 'smoke bush' inflorescences. When they do so, it is worth while saving the seed as there is much variation in the colour of the seedlings and, who knows, one day you may find one that will be different and superior and which may be named after you!

The cotinus that appears to win the most applause for autumn effect is *C. americanus*, and I have read some wonderful descriptions of this. However, I have not yet got a plant in my garden and cannot think it can possibly surpass Notcutt's Variety for all-the-year-round effect. I have seen one growing locally that I should regard as being no better for autumn colour than the ordinary *Rhus typhina*.

That seems to me to be the chief trouble with ignorance in gardening. You read about plants in books and decide that you must have them. You purchase specimens about 6 inches high from the nurseryman and are not impressed. Then, 20 years later, when you decide you quite like them, why, then you have almost missed the boat. I have learned much more about shrubs and trees since I have visited gardens opened to the public by kind owners, but am pained by the fact that I no longer have the space to grow all the treasures I see.

PLANTS REFERRED TO IN THIS CHAPTER

Name	*Origin of species*	*Ultimate height and spread*	*Description*	*Annual rate of growth in author's garden*
Berberis thunbergii	Japan	4ft. × 5ft.	Glorious autumn colour.	6–8in.
atropurpurea		4ft. × 5ft.	Purple foliage and good autumn colour.	6–8in.
nana		2ft. × 3ft.		3–4in.
wilsonae	W. Szechwan	3ft. × 3ft.	Coral-red berries in autumn. Mind the prickles!	6–8in.
Chaenomeles				
speciosa	Japan	3ft. × 5ft.	Scarlet flowers in spring.	3–4in.
moerloesii		7ft. × 7ft.	Pink and white flowers in spring.	
nivalis		7ft. × 7ft.	White flowers in spring.	
rosea flore pleno		7ft. × 7ft.	Double rose-pink flowers in spring.	
Rowallane Seedling		7ft. × 7ft.	Scarlet-crimson flowers.	12–18in.
superba Knap Hill Scarlet		7ft. × 7ft.	Scarlet flowers in spring.	
Cotinus				
americanus	S.E. United States	8ft. × 8ft.	Attractive foliage and good autumn colour.	12in.
coggygria foliis purpureis		6ft. × 10ft.	Retains its smoky inflorescences for weeks.	6–9in.
Notcutt's Variety		6ft. × 10ft.	Looks wonderful with grey-leaved shrubs and with *Lobelia cardinalis* Queen Victoria.	6–9in.

Name	*Origin of species*	*Ultimate height and spread*	*Description*	*Annual rate of growth in author's garden*
Cotoneaster adpressus praecox		2–3ft. high, goes on spreading.	Very attractive wavy-edged leaves and large red berries.	12–18in.
frigidus	Himalaya	15ft. × 15ft.	Autumn berries and more of a small tree than a bush.	12–24in.
horizontalis	China	3ft. × 8ft.	The Fishbone Cotoneaster.	12–24in.
variegatus		3ft. × 8ft.	An attractive variegated form.	
microphyllus	Himalaya	6–12in. high, but spreads indefinitely.	Small leaves, ¼ to ½in. long.	6–12in.
thymifolius		6–12in. × 10ft.	Suitable for the rock garden.	6–12in.
salicifolius floccosus		16ft. × 10ft.	The Willow-leaved Cotoneaster. Graceful shrub with red berries.	12–24in.
Cytisus				
albus	Spain and Portugal	6–12ft. × 6ft.	White flowers in May/June.	
praecox		4ft. × 4ft.	Cream flowers in May. Rather unpleasant scent.	12–18in.
scoparius	W. Europe	8ft. × 5ft.	Rapid growth.	12–18in.
Daphne mezereum	Europe	4ft. × 3ft.	Flowers in shades of reddish-mauve February/March. Delightful perfume. Red berries.	4–6in.
alba			White flowers and yellow berries.	3–4in.
Forsythia Beatrix Farrand		8ft. × 6ft.	New variety with large yellow flowers.	12–18in.
intermedia spectabilis		8ft. × 6ft.	Each shoot packed with bright golden flowers in April.	12–18in.
Lynwood		8ft. × 6ft.	New variety said to be the best yet.	12–18in.
suspensa	E. China	8ft. × 10ft.	The best forsythia for walls.	12–18in.
fortunei		8ft. high	Covers a terrific area as it layers itself. Beware of bullfinches and sparrows. They love all the forsythias.	12–18in.
viridissima	E. China	8ft. × 8ft.	Not one of the best.	12–18in.

Name	Origin of species	Ultimate height and spread	Description	Annual rate of growth in author's garden
Philadelphus				
Belle Etoile		6ft. × 6ft.	Single white flowers with central maroon flush.	6–12in.
coronarius aureus		6ft. × 8ft.	Bright yellow leaves in the spring.	
Innocence		6ft. × 8ft.	Leaves have creamy-white variegation.	
microphyllus	WesternNorth America	3ft. × 3ft.	Single white flowers in June.	3–12in.
Virginal		8ft. × 5ft.	Double white flowers in June. Delightfully fragrant.	12–18in.
Rhus typhina	E. North America	10ft. × 8ft.	Attractive foliage and good autumn colour.	12–18in.
Ribes				
odoratum	W. North America	6ft. × 6ft.	Scented yellow flowers in April.	
sanguineum albidum		6ft. × 6ft.	Pale dreary flowers in April.	12–18in.
King Edward VII		4ft. × 5ft.	Red flowers in April.	12–18in.
Pulborough Scarlet		9ft. × 9ft.	Red flowers in April.	12–18in.
splendens		6ft. × 6ft.	Red flowers in April.	12–18in.
speciosum	California	6ft. × 5ft.	Red flowers like small fuchsias in April and May.	
Rubus				
deliciosus	Rocky Mountains	6ft. × 4ft.	Single white flowers in May.	6–12in.
Tridel		6ft. × 4ft.	An improved hybrid.	
Santolina chamaecyparissus	Mediterranean	1½ft. × 1½ft.	The Lavender Cotton, with decorative grey foliage.	6in.
Spartium junceum	,,	10ft. × 10ft.	Yellow flowers from July to September. Grows straggly unless clipped to shape.	12–24in.
Spiraea				
arguta		6ft. × 8ft.	Branches wreathed with small white flowers in May.	12–18in.
bumalda Anthony Waterer		3ft. × 3ft.	Rosy-red flowers July to August.	6–9in.
japonica alba		3ft. × 3ft.	White flowers July to August.	
thunbergii	China, Japan	4ft. × 4ft.	Very dainty foliage and small white flowers April to May.	6–9in.

Name	*Origin of species*	*Ultimate height and spread*	*Description*	*Annual rate of growth in author's garden*
Syringa Katherine Havemeyer		12ft. × 15ft.	Purplish-lavender flowers in May/June. Growth variable according to the age of the shrub.	1–2ft.
Madame Lemoine		12ft. × 15ft.	Very free-flowering double white.	1–2ft.
Souvenir de Louis Spath		12ft. × 15ft.	A very fine variety. Dark red single flowers in May/June.	1–2ft.
Weigela florida foliis purpureis		6ft. × 6ft.	Slow-growing compact shrub with purple foliage and pink flowers in May/June.	
variegata		8ft. × 5ft.	Pale pink flowers May/June, attractive variegated foliage.	12–18in.
middendorffiana	N. China	4ft. × 4ft.	Sulphur yellow flowers, stained with orange on the lower lobes, April/May. Not as hardy as the previous two varieties.	

CHAPTER FOUR

More Shrubs

... yes, in spite of all,
Some shape of beauty moves away the pall
From our dark spirits.
John Keats

As the finest winter-flowering shrub, I give pride of place to the Witch-hazel, *Hamamelis mollis*. We are constantly being told about shrubs for winter effect, only to find on trying them that winter has extended into spring. My idea of a winter-flowering plant is one that is giving a display amid the ice and snow of January, and I do not mean the odd flower here and there. *H. mollis* fulfils these qualifications. Bought over 25 years ago for the sum of 6 shillings, my specimen is now well over 10 feet high. It is rather a lanky looking shrub and was installed before I had learned how to treat such treasures. It was carelessly planted in ordinary garden soil, no peat or humus of any kind being incorporated and, quite frankly, the results have astonished me.

When my Witch-hazel was quite small I well remember going out into the garden and digging down into the snow to look at the yellow filaments, which are its petals, to find them completely unharmed by the cold proximity of the ice. And what a delightful perfume it has! It drifts lavishly upon the air on the occasional mild sunny day in late December or early January. When recklessness overtakes me, I gather small twigs of this charmer and put them in the Christmas bowls of flowers from the garden, but never do I prune it otherwise, and the only rewards I give it for its unfailing bounty are my blessing and the peat mulch it so richly earns.

The price of this plant has risen steeply since the time of my original purchase, but anyone who has tried to get a layering from this choicest of winter-flowering shrubs will gladly pay the sum demanded. Nurserymen's prices may seem high on occasions, but a good specimen plant of any kind is well worth the money spent upon it. I never cease to be amazed at the sums of money some people expend on the weekly purchase of cut flowers and at the astonishment these same people show when they are told the price of a shrub that will give years of pleasure.

As the Witch-hazel was doing so well, I thought I would like to extend my knowledge of this interesting family and bought a plant of *H. faponica arborea*. This was a most disappointing shrub compared with its Chinese relative and, after struggling on for a number of years, eventually it died.

When I am looking round the garden for winter flowers for the house, my search invariably takes me down the shrubbery. If the weather has been mild, I can usually find a few twigs of *Prunus subhirtella autumnalis* and, if I am fortunate, a few opening heads of *Viburnum jragrans*. This last is a well-named plant, as the flowers have a most heavenly fragrance and can often be found in bloom well before Christmas. Unlike those of the Witch-hazel, however, they are destroyed by the first hint of frost and although the shrub grows quite well here, it rarely produces a good display and I must reluctantly conclude that it is not a plant for a cold climate.

I have attempted to grow many of the so-called winter-flowering shrubs but these are the only ones I find actually flowering in the middle of winter, that is, in December and January, apart from the ericas and, of course, the Jasmine. The others are either not hardy or flower later.

I have mentioned dogwoods or cornus in Chapter Two, for growing in association with silver birches. I have planted several specimens of the Cornelian Cherry, *Cornus mas*, at different times, as I thought it would make a good follow-on for the Witch-hazel. However, it has just been another failure and dwindles away.

Cornus kousa, with the very showy bracts, has been in the garden for several years and, again, has hardly grown at all. I think that the climate must either be too dry for it or that it is a slow starter. I have found this to be the case with many of the shrubs I have planted. Some of them remain dormant for years and then, suddenly, just after one has given them an awful warning to pull up their socks, or else, away they go, surpassing even one's most sanguine expectations. This, naturally, makes one extremely wary of making snap judgments.

There is another dogwood which can hardly be called a shrub, but which is doing so well that I feel obliged to mention it. This is *C. canadensis*, the Creeping Dogwood, no more than 6 inches high; a most useful carpeting plant for the woodland and one of distinct quality. It has survived the severest winters without the slightest injury and, in mild ones, has retained its crimson autumn-tinted leaves. *C. canadensis* has small, creamy-white, four-petalled flowers about the size of a halfpenny, that are produced in summer and, again, sporadically, in the autumn. These are succeeded by bunches of shiny bright red berries, rather like those used in the olden days for trimming ladies' hats. Unfortunately they do not persist for long, falling within a week or so. I had thought that they might be succulent morsels for the birds or mice, but found them on the surface of the soil hidden by the foliage. The pairs of opposite leaves of the Creeping Dogwood are alternate on the stems, so that when one looks down on them the four-petalled theme of the flowers appears to be repeated.

When I first bought my specimen it came in a pot, so I just put the contents into a well-prepared hole, not bothering to disturb the roots. As I did so I must have noticed that these were growing in spiral formation because, as the plant did not seem to be doing much during its first year, I thought I would fork it up and have a look. In consequence, I unravelled the roots and was astonished to find that they extended for about 18 inches. I re-planted them laterally and have found that my *C. canadensis* has now thrown suckers all along the length of the roots and is continuing to spread by a thicket of stems. It is easy to propagate; small suckers of about 2 inches in height root quickly in a pot of sandy, peaty loam. I give my plant a mulch of peat in the spring and it seems to appreciate this. Many plants received from the nurseries are pot-bound and my experience with my dogwood has taught me to unravel the roots of such specimens before planting them in their permanent positions.

Several years ago I received a packet of seeds from Wisley labelled *Enkianthus chinensis.* This was the luck of the draw and I had no idea then of the nature of the plant. However, I sowed the seeds and, to my surprise, a large number of them germinated. By this time, of course, I had ascertained that they were ericaceous, that is acid-loving, and quite scarce into the bargain. The foliage of these shrubs grows in tiers rather in the manner of the Ghent azaleas, and the heather-like flowers hang down from the stems in clusters and are salmon-red. These are followed by brightly coloured red berries, while, in the autumn, the leaves turn magnificent shades of orange and red. I had not realised, until I saw some specimens in another garden, that these plants show off better when put in a raised border, so that you can look up into the bushes. They are woodland shrubs, preferring semi-shade, eventually growing to about 6 feet in height. They are distinctly hardy, of fairly rapid growth, and while to the enthusiast they have great appeal, to the amateur they may not be flamboyant enough. Need I mention that they are easily propagated by seed?

Years ago someone kindly bought me a florist's hydrangea as a present, and, of course, it found its way into the garden. There it stood, year after year, every winter cut almost to ground level by frost. My optimism led me to the false hope that one year it would surprise me by flowering, but all it did was to produce an abundance of new wood. And then I went to Bodnant in North Wales and saw those spectacular blue hydrangeas growing on the terraces and in the woods. My enthusiasm was fired. I was determined to see whether I could trace this variety and obtain similar results. Eventually I secured a plant under the name of *Hydrangea macrophylla hortensia* Générale Vicomtesse de Vibraye. This hydrangea flowers from the buds on the lateral shoots as well as from those on the terminal ones, which means that if the terminal buds are destroyed by the severity of the winter or by spring frosts, the plant will produce flowers on the laterals. If you live on an acid soil, you will get those exciting blue flowers. In the frost hole which is my garden, even so Vibraye is not always covered with bloom, but in a more elevated position higher up the hill, my neighbour's plants, growing in full exposure, have not yet failed to give a magnificent display.

Over the years I have been trying some of the other varieties said to flower from the buds on their lateral shoots, such as Ami Pasquier, Madame Mouillière, and Westfalen, but so far have found none of them nearly as good as my first choice, Générale Vicomtesse de Vibraye.

Hydrangeas are easily propagated from young 3-inch shoots taken off and put round the edge of a pot of sandy soil, and when you take large numbers of these every year to give to your friends, as I do, the results are quite interesting. There is no better plant for testing the acidity or alkalinity of your soil than a hydrangea of the *macrophylla* type. On alkaline soils the flowers are pink or red and on acid soils blue or violet. Many times I have given a Vibraye to one of my friends, only to be told in a roundabout, or not so roundabout, way that he did not think much of the colour. 'Thought you said it was blue. Mine's turned an awful wishy-washy pink,' and so on. I am not a bit surprised. Some time ago I put cuttings from a particularly good blue specimen of this variety into pots for house decoration. Thinking to bring them on and assist them in the production of a large number of plump flowering buds, I not only incorporated dried blood into the potting medium, but also fed them with the stuff. When eventually they did come into flower, they were a really glorious pink! Conclusion, if you want your hydrangeas blue, do not feed them with dried blood. If you are gardening on alkaline soil you will, of course, have to use colourant anyway to get blue flowers. Of recent years I have been using pig manure and shavings on some of my older plants and they are a wonderful blue, but it is surprising how the colour can vary even within a small area.

The Lace-cap hydrangeas do not seem nearly as floriferous as the *hortensia* varieties. Severe winters do considerable damage to the wood and they do not appear to flower from the buds on their lateral shoots. I have the varieties Blue Wave and White Wave but rarely get more than one or two heads of bloom on my enormous plants in this low-lying position. At a higher elevation they grow well and I am always rather annoyed when I see my cuttings flowering away locally. However, my Lace-caps look so healthy with their fine, glossy green leaves that I have not had the courage to make a final parting. In any case, they make lovely stock plants and if I want flowers I can always get them by growing a few specimens in pots.

Hydrangea serrata and *H. s.* Grayswood have been attempted and can be counted among my total losses.

Hydrangea paniculata grandiflora has been tried too, but died out after flowering well for a number of years. I had three bushes so it would appear that this variety is not long lived. This seems curious when the *hortensia* type persist so long. I have replaced them with *H. arborescens grandiflora.* So far only one of the three specimens has flowered. It appears to be a weak-growing plant and I am not at all optimistic about its future here. I much prefer the ones I had, although if I do get any more I shall buy the earlier flowering form, *H. paniculata praecox.*

The species that I should like to grow really well is *H. villosa,* a hydrangea with very hairy leaves and stems. I saw a beautiful specimen of this growing against a wall in north Yorkshire many years ago and this gave me the enthusiasm to try to grow it from seed. Unfortunately, even when over-wintered in a cold greenhouse the young plants died, and I more or less forgot about this species until I saw a most lovely bush again about a year ago. So, of course, I bought another plant and in the autumn it produced two trusses of its exquisite lavender-mauve flowers. This is not to say that it is reliably hardy here by any means. That winter was an exceptionally mild one and may not be repeated for years. I have managed to obtain a cutting from my new plant and shall coddle it under glass through the winter.

Before you plant hydrangeas, prepare the soil well. They are vigorous growers and gross feeders and, if they are producing massive heads of bloom, they require the necessary sustenance. If they are blue with you, then a mulch of peat and animal manure will not only feed them but intensify the colour. If they are a pale pink, rather than try to turn them blue, it may be advisable to try to intensify the pink by using such fertilisers as bonemeal and dried blood. Plant them in the moistest position you have to offer, excluding a bog of course. They are said to prefer a heavy turf loam. Try to see that they are not in full sun for the whole of the day as, if they are, you will find that the flowers wilt, and the petals dry and turn brown in patches, so that the whole effect is ruined. If you live in a frost hole, then you will get much better results if you can find your shrubs the protection of a wall. Some of my best specimens are at the foot of the house wall facing west, but this means that in time of drought they have to be watered. I never give my large plants less than 4 gallons of water each at a time and they seem to absorb this amount within a couple of days. In good years *H.* Générale Vicomtesse de Vibraye gives a floral display from July until the first hard frosts. It is not recommended that the flower heads are removed before the winter is over, as these afford protection for the terminal buds. However, the occasional one may be picked and dried for winter decoration, for which purpose they are admirably suited.

My early experience with my florists' hydrangea gave me a totally misleading impression of these plants for garden decoration, an impression that took years to eradicate. I now consider them to be first-rate garden shrubs, providing throughout the summer masses of colour with a minimum of attention and, if I lived in a hilly district, I should concentrate on growing more of them as they are windproof into the bargain. The most important thing to remember when buying them is to procure the varieties that flower on their lateral shoots.

Many of us love the fuchsias, but find that they are too tender to grow in the open garden. But there is one variety that may be planted without the slightest risk of loss. Admittedly the flowers are very much smaller, but the grace of the plants is such that this is a minor detail. This is *Fuchsia magellanica riccartonii*, often used for hedges. Cut to ground level each winter it may be, but it soon sprouts up again and makes a good dwarf bush for late summer effect. Grown against a wall it makes a lovely and much taller specimen. The paler-flowered form, *F. m. alba*, appears equally hardy. I have recently planted the pretty *F. m. gracilis versicolor* against a west wall in the hope that it will live through the winter, but have taken the precaution of rooting some cuttings which I shall keep under glass. Fuchsias are easily rooted from young 2-inch shoots removed with a heel, and the cuttings will flower freely during the first year of their lives. I have attempted to grow several of the larger flowered hybrids in the open, but in spite of protection in the way of bracken or fern fronds, they have not survived the Yorkshire winters. Someone has suggested that the secret is to bury the roots more deeply so I must try this method of planting.

Deutzia scabra plena was one of the early introductions to the shrubbery. I had read much about its hardiness and was attracted by the illustrations of its beautiful panicles of flowers. As a matter of fact I never even saw a flower during the whole of the 15 years it was in the garden, as the buds were consistently frost-nipped. In the end my three bushes of well over 6 feet high were dug up and consigned to the bonfire, as their habit alone was not good enough to justify their retention. Note: do not attempt this shrub in low lying gardens having late spring frosts.

As a postscript and to illustrate the pure pig-headedness of the dedicated gardener, I must tell you that I have just bought another variety, *D. rosea carminea*, which I have admired for a number of years. I intend to plant it against a sunny wall and keep my fingers crossed.

Of all the viburnums I have grown, none gives me greater pleasure than that supreme variety *Viburnum tomentosum* Lanarth. This is a large shrub of tabular form, ideal for placing on a corner where something is needed to impress. The tiers of its branches reach to at least 7 feet and in May and June the length of each one of them is covered with cream umbels of flowers, rather in the style of the Lacecap hydrangeas. Sometimes the blossom is touched by the late spring frosts, but the bush itself remains unharmed. Birds love to nest among its branches, which provide such dense cover that you only find the nests when the wrinkled green leaves have fallen. To retain a flattened dome-shaped appearance, any branches growing vertically should be snipped off. This can be done during the summer months. This viburnum has a most vigorous surface rooting system, as you will discover when you try to dig up any of its numerous layers and, in consequence, it appreciates a mulch, either in the form of bonfire ash, peat or well-rotted manure. In the autumn its leaves turn to indescribable shades of purplish-russet and dull gold. No plant in the garden surpasses this one from the point of view of habit, flower, autumn tints or ease of propagation, but it should be given plenty of space. There is only one thing that I can say to its detriment: the flowers are scentless.

Recently I have planted a specimen of *V. t.* Rowallane. This has more rounded leaves than Lanarth and is said to be a less vigorous variety, in which case it would probably be a better choice for a small garden. I have been told also that the display of berries in the autumn is almost as attractive as that of the flowers in the spring.

I cannot report much success with *V. carlesii.* My specimen was a grafted plant, perpetually addicted to blackfly and an extremely bad doer, eventually being overcome by the stock on which it was grafted. Wonderfully fragrant as the flowers of these shrubs unquestionably are, mine was a complete failure and I have not obtained a replacement. The well-known Snowball Bush, *V. opulus sterile*, succumbed to blackfly and was thrown on the bonfire. I am left wondering why birds refuse to tackle these infernal little insects.

For many years I grew the shrubby cinquefoils, potentillas, and was not over-impressed. Each winter they retreated into their own black drabness, never seeming to come into bloom until nearly every other shrub in the garden was over, and flowering so sparsely that eventually I threw them out as not earning their keep. Then I read about *Potentilla arbuscula* and, wanting some late colour in the garden, decided to have another try. Ideal for the smaller plot, this potentilla blooms non-stop from June to October, literally covering itself with large yellow flowers. It is the perfect shrub for rock gardens, tubs or jardinières, forming a rather spreading bush of about 3 feet in height. So impressed have I been with its performance that I have planted the form *P. a.* Kingdon-Ward. This is a shrub of more erect growth, having a larger and much deeper-coloured yellow flower, but I do not think it is going to bloom as freely as the type. The stems of this plant are interesting, being chestnut brown in colour, the shoots emerging from papery brown sheaths.

Both of these shrubby cinquefoils are readily propagated from shoots pulled off with a heel in the summer and placed round the edge of a pot of sandy soil and covered with a polythene bag until the cuttings are seen to be growing.

Several years ago I saw a most unusual shrub that I felt I must attempt to grow. This was *Decaisnea fargesii.* The yellowish-green flowers grow in racemes up to 18 inches in length and are followed by pod-like blue fruits 3 to 4 inches long. While it is quite hardy here I think it would be better in a more elevated position, as the young foliage is frost-tender. This year, in the absence of late spring frost, it has grown extremely well and I am waiting anxiously to see whether it is going to flower and fruit for me. Whether it does or not, it is still a handsome shrub with attractive pinnate leaves.

If you are searching for a tropical-looking foliage plant for a formal effect, then *Yucca recurvifolia* may suit you. Yuccas require full sun and good drainage and although I find them difficult to place in this garden, I always fancy that the best position for them is in a raised bed near a flagged path close to the house, where you can look up into the beautiful creamy-white blooms. It is a fallacy to believe that all yuccas flower only once every seven years. This species does so nearly every year, in July, the fat flower heads forcing their way up from the centres of the plants. It is said that in their native home, the Southern United States, they have their own special moth to fertilise the blossoms.

Yucca gloriosa

Certainly we do not have it here, as the seeds never set and one has to rely upon the inexhaustible supply of small plants which spring up from the tuberous roots.

Someone once gave me a *Y. gloriosa*, which, to my astonishment, regularly threw up a flower stem in the middle of winter. I thought I had seen the last of it in the winter of 1962, but no, a small plant reappeared two years later. These shrubs are called Adam's Needles, and if you have ever put your finger on the tip of one of the leaves you will appreciate why. I always think it exceedingly unwise to grow yuccas where there are young children playing about in the garden.

It will have been noticed that many of the plants that I have described and said that I have lost have not been replaced. One of the rules that I have taken to heart is never to defy the forces of Nature. If plants die on you when you have planted them well, do not replace them, but find something that will grow in their stead. I except evergreens from this generalisation, as we, in this part of the country, must struggle with them. If any sort of garden is to be achieved, they cannot be dispensed with.

PLANTS REFERRED TO IN THIS CHAPTER

Name	*Origin of species*	*Ultimate height and spread*	*Description*	*Annual rate of growth in author's garden*
Cornus				
canadensis	N. America	8–10in. spreading indefinitely	Creamy-white flowers in June followed by red berries.	Spreads about 12–18in.
kousa	Japan, Korea	20ft. × 20ft.	Creamy-white bracts in June.	3–6in.
mas	Europe	20ft. × 25ft.	Yellow bracts in February/March.	
Decaisnea fargesii	W. China	10–12ft. × 6ft.	Yellowish-green flowers in June followed by pod-like metallic blue fruits.	9–12in.
Deutzia rosea carminea		4ft. × 4ft.	Pinkish-mauve flowers in June.	12–18in.
scabra plena		10ft. × 6ft.	Double white flowers in June, frost-tender.	Rapid 12–18in.
Enkianthus chinensis	Central and W. China	8ft. × 6ft.	Salmon-red flowers in May followed by red berries. Wonderful autumn tints. Peat loving.	12–15in.
Fuchsia				
magellanica alba		6ft. × 6ft.	Graceful shrub flowering from July onwards. White flowers faintly tinged mauve.	24–36in.

Dodecatheon meadia. A shady, moist but well-drained position will help this plant to produce, without difficulty, its purplish-pink flowers with golden eyes

The cascade of flowers shown in this illustration belongs to *Campanula portenschlagiana;* their blue and white colouring emphasises the impression of water

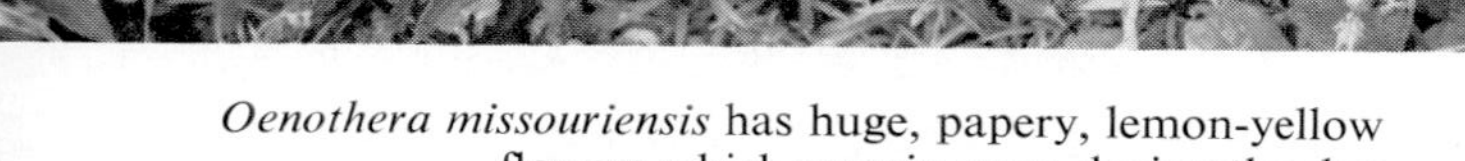

Oenothera missouriensis has huge, papery, lemon-yellow flowers which remain open during the day

The blue-grey dwarf conifer *Juniperus communis compressa*

Name	*Origin of species*	*Ultimate height and spread*	*Description*	*Annual rate of growth in author's garden*
Fuchsia				
gracilis versicolor		3ft. × 3ft.	Leaves grey-green, variegated pink, crimson and cream.	18–24in.
riccartonii		6ft. × 6ft.	Flowers of scarlet and purple.	24–36in.
Hamamelis japonica				
arborea		15ft. × 12ft.	Sweetly scented yellow flowers from January/ March.	
mollis	China	12ft. × 15ft.	Yellow sweetly scented flowers from December/ January. A wonderful winter-flowering shrub.	6–9in.
Hydrangea arborescens				
grandiflora		4ft. × 4ft.	Cream flowers from July onwards.	12–18in.
macrophylla			Crimson or French blue.	6–12in.
Ami Pasquier		2ft. × 2ft.	August.	
Blue Wave		4–6ft. × 6ft.	Lacecap type, pink or blue. August.	24–36in.
Générale Vicomtesse de Vibraye		3ft. × 5ft.	Blue or pink. Never fails to produce flowers even when cut to ground level in the winter. The best outdoor variety.	18–30in.
Madame Mouillière		3–4ft. × 3–4ft.	White flowers with either a pink or blue eye.	18–24in.
Westfalen		1–2ft. × 1–2ft.	Ink blue or pure crimson.	6–12in.
White Wave		4–6ft. × 6ft.	Lacecap, blue or pink fertile flowers surrounded by white ray-flowers.	24–36in.
paniculata grandiflora		4–6ft. × 4ft.	Massive panicles of creamy sterile florets in August. Very showy.	12–18in.
praecox		4–6ft. × 4ft.	A July-flowering form.	
serrata Grayswood		3ft. × 3ft.	Inflorescence blue with white ray florets changing to deep crimson.	
villosa	China	9ft. × 9ft.	Glorious bluish-mauve inflorescences with pale blue ray florets. August/ September. Slugs love it!	12in.

Name	*Origin of species*	*Ultimate height and spread*	*Description*	*Annual rate of growth in author's garden*
Potentilla				
arbuscula	Himalaya and N. China	3ft. × 4ft.	Large yellow flowers from June/October. Quite the best potentilla in my garden.	Up to 9in.
Kingdon Ward		3ft. × 4ft.	Bright yellow flowers. Chestnut brown stems.	Up to 15in.
Viburnum				
carlesii	Korea	5ft. × 5ft.	Gloriously fragrant white flowers, April/May.	Slow
fragrans	China	10ft. × 10ft.	Pinkish-white flowers from November onwards.	6–9in.
opulus sterile		12ft. × 12ft.	The Snowball Tree. White flowers in globose heads. June.	
tomentosum Lanarth Variety		10ft. × 10ft.	Wide-spreading horizontal branches. White flowers in May, June. Good autumn colour.	12–24in.
Rowallane		6ft. × 6ft.	A much smaller shrub than Lanarth with the same virtues.	6–12in.
Yucca				
gloriosa	S.E. United States	6ft. × 6ft. high	White flowers July to September.	
recurvifolia	Southern United States	6ft. × 6ft.	The easiest of the yuccas. Flowers nearly every year in this garden.	6in.

CHAPTER FIVE

Rhododendrons, Azaleas and Heathers

Fill'd with the face of heaven, which, from afar,
Comes down upon the waters; all its hues,
From the rich sunset to the rising star,
Their magical variety diffuse:

Byron

And now we come to the rhododendrons, a vexed question indeed in an area of low rainfall and heavily polluted atmosphere. Of course I like them. I think that their form is indispensable in garden design and, if you can get colour as well, then you must have them. But, oh dear, where to begin? If you live in the sort of district that I live in you must forget about making them the most important plants in your garden. Cross out the names of most of them, except the ones that are indestructibly hardy unless, of course, you are prepared to take risks, as most enthusiasts are. On the credit side, be glad that you will never get bitten by the 'rhododendron bug', which is apt to blind you to the merits of any other type of shrub.

Who is not absolutely enthralled by the sight of a well-grown bush of *Rhododendron* Lady Chamberlain, shall we say, when it is carrying a crop of those most beautiful, drooping, narrow, bell-shaped flowers of peachy-orange? Or by the glaucous blue foliage of the species *R. thomsonii*, set against the blood-red of its bell-shaped blooms, or by the leaves of the magnificent Himalayan rhododendrons, sometimes as much as 30 inches long, with rust-coloured, tomentose undersurface? Or, for that matter, by the rounded, heart-shaped leaves of the frost-tender *R. williamsianum*? And so I could go on. But, for me, these are but the stuff of dreams, probably of a garden in Heaven, to which I shall be refused admittance. No matter. I know that these treasures exist and that I must live without them. I must learn to appreciate the varieties of rhododendron that will grow in this discouraging gardening area, grumbling less about their comparatively unattractive features. After all, no plant can do more than try to please.

If you garden on limestone, it is better to forget about rhododendrons altogether, as there are only one or two that are lime-tolerant. I am one of those gardeners who know that plants are living beings, not just in the sense of growing, but almost in a sense of awareness, and I am not a bit surprised to read of the experiments of American scientists that prove that they can almost talk too! I am sure that a number of plants I have introduced to the garden have almost sworn at me for asking them to exist in unsuitable conditions, and have shown their disapproval by dying without even bothering to open their eyes. What a blessing it is that there are some of sturdier clay! Of course, soil can be chemically treated nowadays, and ways can be found of growing plants in unsuitable conditions, but the lazy gardener is not inclined to make this sort of effort.

To the uninitiated, and for their information alone, let me say that the Royal Horticultural Society issues a *Rhododendron Handbook* in which are listed rhododendrons placed in categories according to their hardiness and cultural requirements. At the top of the list, for all-round hardiness and suitability for inclusion in most gardens, are what are coded as the H^4 varieties, and these are the ones that present the least difficulty in my Yorkshire garden. All those species and varieties listed at the end of this chapter are included in this category with the exception of *R. augustinii*, *R. campylocarpum*, *R. pemakoense*, *R. williamsianum* and *R.* Lady Chamberlain, which are all rated H^{3-4} in the *Handbook*. The classification H^3 indicates that a species is hardy in the South and West, along the seaboard and in a sheltered garden inland, and H^{3-4} that some forms of the species in question are represented by H^3 and others by H^4.

Most of the hybrids in this category flower towards the end of May and at the beginning of June, when the danger of spring frost is receding. They may look dirty, bedraggled and pinched for three or four months of the year, sometimes they may be partly defoliated too during the winter, but if you have a selection which includes such varieties as Countess of Athlone, frilly-petalled, mauve; Cynthia, rosy-crimson; *R. fastuosum flore pleno*, double blue-mauve; Gomer Waterer, blush; John Walter, rosy-crimson; Lady Clementine Mitford, peach-pink; Madame de Bruin, cerise-red, and Purple Splendour, deep purple, you will be sure of a display. To my surprise, the white-flowered rhododendron Mrs A. T. de la Mare, which was sent to me as a substitute for another variety, and is in category H^3 in the *Handbook*, has done as well for me as the H^4 varieties.

I am often asked how to group rhododendrons and azaleas. To begin with I am not in favour of a preponderance of strong colours, but think that scarlets, crimsons and deep purples should be used as highlights in groupings of paler shades. The mauves, whites, soft yellows and purples look well together, while alternatively crimson may be the highlight in a planting of pink, white and pale yellow.

Among the rhododendron species, *R. augustinii* is the one that I would choose to grow. In its best forms it is a most enchanting blue and the sight of a large group of these plants is something to remember. I was given some seedlings recently and am hoping to get them on by keeping them under glass during the winter until they are slightly larger, when I shall put them into permanent positions in the open garden, in the most protected place I can find, beneath a canopy of trees. As *R. augustinii* is in category H^4, it should be quite hardy here, but as it flowers in May when spring frosts are frequent, it is doubtful whether it will bloom regularly, if at all.

I have been testing *R. campylocarpum*, too, for about five years, in the hope that this glorious yellow-flowered species might find the conditions to its liking. It was a very tiny plant when it arrived from the nursery and has hardly grown at all, but at least it is alive. *R. haematodes* is another small plant in my collection and, again, is in category H^4. So far it has not produced any of its red flowers, but I am attracted by the dense brown indumentum (a felt-like growth of hairs) on the underside of the leaves. It appears to be quite hardy but of slow growth. *R. orbiculare* has flowered several times since it was introduced to the garden and seems to escape the spring frosts in some years. It has lovely pink flowers. When the foliage is damaged by the frost it quickly produces secondary growth, and the shape of the leaves is so appealing that I am prepared to put up with the loss of bloom.

If the weather is kind the hybrid *R. praecox* flowers for me, but I am afraid it gets caught by the frost more often than not. In a more elevated position locally it is quite satisfactory, and I see quite a number of these engaging shrubs of between 2 and 3 feet high growing on the outskirts of the neighbouring town. I also have some seedlings of *R. yunnanense* which have now budded up well. This species makes rapid growth and my seed was taken from a plant growing less than 2 miles away. I have an idea that I read recently that someone was having difficulty in getting his plants to flower, but this does not seem to be a problem with my neighbour's specimen.

One of my favourites is *R. russatum*, with an ultimate height of between

3 and 4 feet. Here is a good-tempered shrub indeed. It has already been moved three times during its brief career with me, but has not yet missed giving a wonderful display of its deep violet-purple flowers each spring.

Now there are certain indispensable dwarf rhododendrons that can tolerate almost any conditions as long as you do not ask them to live in calcareous soil and take the trouble to plant them with a few handfuls of peat. My interpretation of this amount has never been less than half a bucketful, and it has paid dividends. In the case of the larger rhododendrons I use about four bucketfuls of peat or leafmould for each specimen.

Rhododendron impeditum is one such small shrub that should be planted in every garden in which it is capable of being grown. It builds itself up into low compact mounds, never failing to produce masses of purplish-blue flowers each spring. There are variable forms of *R. impeditum*, as in most species, some having deeper coloured flowers than others, but whatever shade you get from the nurseryman you will be delighted, as it is a shrub that improves with age. The best specimen I have was trodden on by our large Airedale dog, completely ruining its symmetry, and I remember how disheartened I felt at the time. Now, several years later the bush itself has taken steps to repair the damage, and it would take the eye of an expert to detect the side on which the break occurred.

Those attractive hybrids Blue Tit, Bluebird and Blue Diamond are of slightly looser habit, even in full exposure, than *R. impeditum*, and more susceptible to frost damage. They are all placed in category H^4, with flowers approaching that true blue to be found in good specimens of *R. augustinii*. What is gained in the colour of the blooms in these cases, however, is lost in the habit. The choice is yours. As my specimens of these plants are no more than a foot high, after six or seven years, I naturally concluded that they were of the same dwarf stature as *R. impeditum*, why I do not know. Imagine my amazement on reading the label attached to a fine bush of at least 5 feet in height growing in an Irish garden, to find the words Blue Tit. To add insult to injury, it was an extremely good colour too, being of a much darker blue than the ones in this garden. *Rhododendron fastigiatum* seems almost identical to *R. impeditum*, but is lankier in habit. These small rhododendrons all seem to grow into more compact bushes if grown in full sun and exposure. If grown in the shade, they become more leggy and less floriferous.

I have recently planted a specimen of *R. scintillans*. The leaves of this are rather narrow and, at the moment, the branches are inclined to straggle. This lavender-blue species is highly regarded by many people so I must wait and see how it develops. *R. hippophaeoides* has also just been acquired. This is said to be one of the most satisfactory of the Chinese rhododendrons for less favourable climates, so that it should be right for me. It grows to an ultimate height of 4 to 5 feet and has lavender-coloured flowers. *R. pemakoense* has the fascinating dodge of running about by means of underground suckers. Last year I was given a plant of this species, with strong recommendations, but have my doubts about its usefulness as its pinkish-purple flowers open in April, and I am afraid that this will be too early to escape frost damage.

I planted the yellow-flowered *R. hanceanum nanum* several years ago, after seeing a flourishing specimen in the garden at Rowallane in Ireland. My small plant was only 2 inches in height when it arrived from the nursery and the foliage has proved extremely frost-tender. So far it has not formed flower buds but when it does I am sure that they will need protection.

Two years ago I bought the variety Carmen. The most distinctive, waxy, bright crimson flowers of this shrub make it easily recognisable, even to the amateur. I have seen some lovely specimens growing in Scotland and while on holiday there found I was getting quite good at identifying this particular variety. So far my own plant has not flowered, although I see that buds have formed for next year. *Rhododendron keleticum* is another little dwarf, forming hummocks of small leaves. This has not flowered for me yet either, but seems to be quite happy on the rock garden where it is layering itself rapidly.

When you plant your rock garden, be sure to include one or two of the smaller rhododendrons, as they make neat, symmetrical evergreens. You will probably have to wait a number of years for a sizeable bush, but these plants are well worth waiting for and are always interesting. My advice is to look round a nursery and choose what you yourself like when these rhododendrons are in flower in April, May or June. There are always lots of them, both species and hybrids, on display at the spring shows and the exhibitors are delighted to offer advice on a suitable selection.

One word of warning. Encouraged by my success with some of the smaller rhododendrons, I have been forming a collection of them over the last few years, included in which is *R. racemosum*, planted two years ago. In one catalogue this species was said to be as hardy as heather, a rather ambiguous remark as some of the heathers I have tried have been far from hardy. The winter of 1962, admittedly severe, cut back my specimen of this plant badly, although I am pleased to say that it is now recovering. In a more exposed position, in a neighbouring garden, it was killed outright.

I will move on to the azaleas, those gorgeous shrubs that form a section of the genus *Rhododendron* and are also lime hating. Their colours are repeated in few other families of plants—fiery reds, oranges, yellows, whites, creams, pinks, salmons, mauves, and the flowers are produced in luxuriant profusion. Not for them the grimy look of the rhododendrons growing in industrial areas, nor the thin, shrivelled winter foliage. There they stand, their branches in tiered formation, just growing. For them no pruning, no spraying, no disbudding. If you are as fond of them as I am, you will certainly give them an annual mulch of peat or fallen leaves, or if you can get hold if it, spent hops from the breweries. I tried to give mine an extra special treat in the way of a handful or two of hoof and horn, but in came a flock of local dogs, like the Pied Piper's rats, sniffing, scratching and digging—disaster to azaleas and rhododendrons—at the foot of the bushes in an attempt to find out what this most mouth-watering scent was. They mostly came under cover of night, while the sleeping watchdog, Daisy, dreamed in her box.

I have had to put Daisy in the chapter associated with these well-loved plants. She is a mongrel, rescued by my husband from the Dogs' Home. My first introduction to her was coming through the garden gate one day and seeing a small, sausage-shaped puppy following him at heel, up and down, up and down, as he mowed the lawn. Not for her the tragedy of being lost again, and since then she has remained, literally, glued to our sides. A more co-operative dog we have never possessed, and I have no doubt that had she been at large when the doggy vandals were at work she would have received them at the gate with a torch in her paw and guided them to the scene of the operations. She has never needed any training. To her the garden is sacrosanct except, and this is a large except, when she sees her arch enemy, a cat.

Never, never, never dig with a fork or a spade among the roots of these wonderful shrubs. Lightly scratch the surface soil if you must or, preferably hand-weed, afterwards mulching with either peat or leaf-mould if you remove any of the soil with the weeds. If you find that you have made a mistake with your colour blending, you can lift the bushes and rearrange them without harm. When you plant, be sure to dig a nice large hole. Put some peat or well-rotted leafmould into it and sit the root ball of the azalea on the top, so that the upper surface is slightly below the level of the surrounding soil. Work a mixture of peaty loam quite firmly round it, tread down and then complete the operation by sprinkling peat on the top of the root ball and in all the remaining crevices. When forking the garden subsequently, try to remember that azaleas and rhododendrons do not like their roots buried deeply underground, so do not throw layers of soil on the top of them.

Buy seedling azaleas if you can, or layered specimens, as these are far more vigorous in growth than grafted plants, throwing up new wood from the base each year. Experience has taught me that an equally effective display may be got from unnamed seedlings of the Knap Hill or Exbury type as from the named varieties and, in this way, a big saving can be effected. If you find that a batch of seedlings does not contain all the colours required, then unnamed plants to colour are also obtainable at a slightly higher price.

If you are a little more ambitious and would like to try growing azaleas from seed yourself, then it is simple to do so. Seed can be purchased from most of the leading growers, but if you have a friend with plants in his garden, see if you can persuade him to part with a few seed capsules from his better coloured specimens at the beginning of the year. Roll these between your palms until the seeds are expressed then, sometime in April, sow them on the surface of moist peat in a plastic box and lightly sprinkle them with sand. Put the lid on the box until the seeds begin to germinate, when the lid should be gradually withdrawn over a period of days. Be sure not to leave your young seedlings exposed to bright sunlight at this stage. Prick out the plants when they are about half an inch high into peaty-sandy soil and keep them under cover the first winter of their lives. The following year plant them in a moist shady spot until they reach sizeable proportions, when they may be put into their permanent positions. They should begin to flower when they are about five years old and you have no idea what a thrill of pride you will get when you mention casually to your friends that you have grown your shrubs from seed.

The first azaleas that I saw growing *en masse* were those at Temple Newsam, near Leeds. These are mainly the *Azalea mollis* (*Rhododendron japonicum*) varieties and for me, and possibly for you, they are not the best ones for the conditions we have to offer. Although I do not consider that the Mollis type of azalea can be beaten for the marvellous range and intensity of their colours, it is a great pity that they flower just that little bit earlier than the species *luteum* and the Ghent and *rustica flore pleno* types. As far as I am concerned, too, I place a black mark against them for their scent, which I find most distasteful.

One of the hardiest and most widely planted azaleas is the species *luteum*, the Honeysuckle azalea which, if rather variable in tone, is always some shade of yellow.

I do not grow the sweetly scented June-flowering species *Rhododendron* (*Azalea*) *occidentale*, but I do have the hybrids Exquisita, apricot, and Irene Koster, blush rose. All the hybrids of *R. occidentale* have delicately coloured and most fragrant flowers.

Among the many other species belonging to the azalea section of the genus *Rhododendron*, *vaseyi*, *mucronatum*, *schlippenbachii*, and *viscosum* are all growing in my garden, while a local garden, not so low lying, has *quinquefolium* and *reticulatum*. *R. kaempferi* Daimio is an ideal azalea for the small plot. It has been growing in my garden for years now, is extremely hardy, and has pale orange flowers appearing in late June.

Some of the species, notably *reticulatum*, *quinquefolium* and *schlippenbachii*, have such decorative foliage that it is almost worth planting them

Rhododendron (*Azalea*) *schlippenbachii*

for the pleasure of looking at their leaves alone. They are all frost-tender and if you wish to grow them in a cold district, you will probably find they will need protection until the danger of frost is over. In speaking of frost damage, there are few seasons when any of my azaleas escape it altogether. The plants are at their most susceptible when the young foliage is just emerging from the buds and it is a heartbreaking sight to see this soft growth turned completely black overnight. This, of course, spells death to the primary growth and the bush is then dependent upon secondary growth for any increase in size. It says much for the toughness of azaleas in general that I have not lost one plant of a deciduous variety. They have terrific recuperative powers and by the end of the season it is impossible to trace any setback they may have had in the spring.

The evergreen azaleas are not reliably hardy in my northern area. In most winters they are subject to bark split. This means that when the plants are frozen, their cells become icy and, when they thaw, the cambium layer is separated from the hard core of the stem, causing the plant to die. To get over this difficulty I grow these enchanting varieties in pots for the house and grow the tougher dwarf rhododendrons in the open garden. A good selection for room decoration would be Hinomayo, clear pink; Hinodegiri, bright crimson; and Palestrina, pure white, with a very faint green tinge.

The azaleas of the *malvatica-kaempferi* group are semi-evergreen and hardier than the evergreen types. They will survive in the open garden but do better for me in pots and are exquisite house-plants. Among my favourites are Anny, orange-red; Alice, pink; Kathleen, deep rose; and John Cairns, dark orange-red. Another favourite of mine for indoors is the salmon-orange Orange Beauty, a Kurume x *kaempferi* hybrid. Plunge the pots containing them in an ash pit for most of the summer, keeping the plants well watered, fed and sprayed overhead occasionally. They will probably need re-potting into a fresh mixture of loam, peat and sand about every other year and I do this when they have finished flowering. Brought into a cold greenhouse for protection at the end of September and into a cool room at about the beginning of February, they should come into flower at the end of March or the beginning of April. Do not push them straight out into the open again when they go out of bloom, but put them into the cold greenhouse or cold frame until the end of May, by which time the frosts should be over. They can then go back into the ash pit until the following autumn.

Most azaleas can be grown in pots in this way. The Mollis varieties are quite suitable, that is, if you can bear the scent of them at close quarters, and they can stay in the ash pit until early spring. Both these and the *malvatica* crosses can often be bought at ridiculously low prices at a well-known store. If you can get them when they are fresh in and pot them up straight away, you should be able to acquire a good stock for a reasonable sum, although do not be too disappointed if some of the evergreen varieties die off unaccountably, as they are sometimes quite tricky to establish.

And now I will come to the most suitable varieties of all the hybrid azaleas for growing in the open garden in cold districts. These include the Ghent, *rustica flore pleno*, Knap Hill and Exbury types. Some of them have double flowers and these should be chosen for the more wind-swept situations. Among these I would select *narcissiflora*, pale yellow, Norma, a beautiful bright pinkish-red, deservedly popular, Freya, salmon, Phoebe, a rather pale sulphur-yellow, and Aida, rose. Of the single flowered ones *A. coccinea speciosa*, tangerine-orange, Fanny, an outstanding pink, and *daviesii*, creamy-white, are particularly good. These, with a few exceptions, are the latest of the azaleas to come into flower.

The Knap Hill azaleas, which are usually in flower a little earlier than the Ghent and *rustica flore pleno* types, miss the worst of the frost as well and, with a wider range of colour, are also outstanding plants for the open garden. Among my favourites are Golden Oriole, bright golden-yellow, with an enormous head of buds and remaining in bloom for weeks; Satan, a dazzling red and prolific in flower; Gog, orange with lovely autumn foliage; Persil, as the name would suggest, a very clean white with golden eye; Knap Hill Yellow, in that scarce, not too golden tone I am always on the watch for in yellows; Harvest Moon, another of my favourite yellows, without a golden flare—but I could go on indefinitely as I find all the varieties lovely.

And finally there is the Exbury strain of these hardy azaleas, among which I will not attempt to pick and choose as they are all so beautiful. The flowers of this type are larger, not always an advantage when growing azaleas in exposed situations, and the colours are more varied, but, in my opinion, the habit of both these and the Knap Hills is not nearly as good as that of the Ghent varieties, due, I would say, to the infusion of *occidentale* blood into the strain. Be that as it may, they are all quite wonderful and if you have a sheltered spot in the garden, where the wind will not damage the petals of their enormous flowers, grow any of them and you will be thrilled.

In addition to the floral display of the azaleas, mention must also be made of the autumn tints assumed by their leaves, producing glorious effects. Even the evergreen varieties have a proportion of highly coloured red leaves.

Heaths and Heathers

I am including heaths and heathers in this chapter because I think they associate well with rhododendrons and azaleas and because most of them must also be grown in acid soil. The *Erica carnea* group is lime tolerant, but even so I always include a few handfuls of peat whatever type of heather I am planting.

So much has been written about these small shrubs that there seems little more to say, but I will sketch a brief outline of my personal choices beginning with the Bell Heathers (*Erica cinerea* and its varieties). These all like a sunny position in the garden and an acid soil, and start flowering in July and August. They come in their legions, in all colours from white to mauve and from pink to red and, as far as I am concerned, the more the better. A few of them have most effective golden foliage, such as Golden Drop and Golden Hue. I also like C. D. Eason, Eden Valley, Lilacina and P. S. Patrick, but then there are none I dislike. As all of them are inclined to become straggly with age, it is most important to clip them over in the spring. These heathers are easy to propagate by pulling off, in July, short, non-flowering shoots of about 2 inches in length, with heel attached. If these are inserted round the edge of a pot filled with a mixture of moist peat and sand and covered with a polythene bag, you will find that they will root within a few weeks.

While the cinereas are still flowering, Lings or Heathers (*Calluna vulgaris* and its varieties) begin to bloom. Here again, these will not tolerate lime in the soil. The earliest to flower here is J. H. Hamilton, a prostrate variety with bright double pink flowers, and a real gem. This is followed by the supreme H. E. Beale, a tall plant with the most amazing sprays of double pink flowers, more mauvish in tone than those of J. H. Hamilton. This is a beauty for cutting, remaining in good condition for weeks.

Among the whites, my first choice is *alba plena*, a fine double, against whose lustrous green foliage the pure white flowers stand out to perfection. The variety *searlei aurea* is an exceptionally fine vigorous plant with outstandingly bright golden foliage. Another golden-leaved calluna is Spitfire. This variety is supposed to turn bright red in the winter, as it may well do in other districts, but so far there is no sign of this happening in my garden.

Probably my favourite among the callunas with coloured foliage is the variety *cuprea.* I consider the rich copper tone particularly outstanding. Another good plant, this time with silver foliage, is Silver Queen. When the mauve flowers are out they make an effective contrast to the leaves.

It would be disastrous if I omitted the variety with the prettiest foliage of all. This is Mrs Pat, and I have the greatest difficulty in keeping up a supply of plants to give to her many admirers. Never growing much more than 9 inches in height, the attraction of Mrs Pat lies in the lovely pink tips to her shoots. These are particularly bright when the growth is fresh and young, but the effect persists for months of the year and I can hardly bear to snip the ends off when I tidy up my plants. I have recently been given a plant of *alba aurea.* Instead of having the pink tips of Mrs Pat, the young shoots of this charming plant have lemon-yellow ones, which make a delightful contrast to the bright green foliage. Unfortunately, the effect does not persist once the new growth has hardened.

One of the best ways for the amateur to propagate the callunas is to layer them. I build up my plants with damp peat, using any discarded hairpins to hold down the shoots I wish to layer, and keeping these in position with small stones. Alternatively, callunas are just as easy to propagate by cuttings in the manner I have outlined for *E. cinerea.*

Several of the hybrid ericas seem to be quite happy with me, including Arthur Johnson, George Rendall, H. Maxwell, Silberschmelze and the *tetralix* variety Con. Underwood.

Erica vagans, or the Cornish Heath, is undoubtedly hardy in spite of its name. My favourites are Mrs D. F. Maxwell and St Keverne, both of which are pink varieties, and the white Lyonesse. These three make up a useful trio. Plants of *E. vagans* eventually become much larger than the types of heath and heather mentioned so far.

Among the Tree Heathers there is one that lived here in perfect condition for over 20 years, until the winter of 1962, when it was cut back to ground level. Even so, it did not die completely. A self-layered branch, which had the protection of the snow, survived and, sprouting from the base, is now again over 2 feet high. This plant is *E. arborea alpina.* Originally it made a beautiful specimen in the shrubbery, growing to about 6 feet in height and maintaining a wonderful block of glossy, bright green foliage throughout the year. I have seen other varieties of the tree heath growing in more favoured gardens, but consider the foliage of these to be in no way superior to that of a well grown specimen of *E. arborea alpina.* A solitary specimen of *E. mediterranea* still survives in the garden, where it has been for many years without flowering.

Erica vagans
Mrs D. F. Maxwell

And now to the winter-flowering group of heathers, *E. carnea* and its varieties. Among those I grow, and they are numerous, I would select King George, *vivellii,* Winter Beauty, Springwood and Springwood Pink. I would also select the cross between *carnea* and *mediterranea* —the rose-coloured *darleyensis.* There is also a golden-foliaged one called *E. c. aurea,* but in this dirty area the golden bit often gets lost in the winter grime and it is not until the spring that it seems to regain the touch of gold. Nevertheless, it is still worth growing as a foliage contrast to the others.

Many writers in different parts of the British Isles seem to be able to say which are the earliest and which are the latest of the *carnea* varieties to flower. Here there does not seem to be too much difference between them. The time of flowering, in any event, depends a great deal upon prevailing climatic conditions and no hard and fast rules can be laid down. In most seasons I should say that *darleyensis* is unquestionably the first, sometimes colouring in the old year, closely followed by that very fine variety King George, then Winter Beauty, then the Springwoods and, finally, *vivellii.* However, on rare occasions I have known King George to lead *darleyensis* by as much as a month.

Erica darleyensis

In these circumstances, and as the pink ones are all more or less the same colour, it seems useless to buy varieties which are supposed to extend the period of flowering.

Both Springwood and Springwood Pink differ from the others in growth, covering the ground much more quickly. They root as they run and are at their best when growing in strong light. When you want

Chionodoxa luciliae, which bears blue flowers with white eyes in the spring

Another spring-flowering plant is *Erythronium dens-canis*, of which there are both pink and white varieties

Narcissus February Gold, a hybrid from *N. cyclamineus* which flowers well and increases rapidly

Galtonia candicans, a bulbous plant which bears its white, green-tinged flowers in late summer

them, as I do, for carpeting the ground beneath shrubs, you will find that they are not so floriferous nor, in the case of Springwood Pink, quite such a strong colour as they are when growing in sunnier positions. No matter, in this day of do-it-yourself, they are the answer to every gardener's prayer.

All the heathers are pretty faultless to me, except that when used for ground cover they do preclude the growing of small bulbs. Crocuses of the more vigorous Dutch types will struggle through the foliage, but the more dwarf bulbs are smothered.

The varieties of *E. carnea* also benefit from regular clipping over after flowering. I found that when we had rabbits in the garden they used to do this for me! These heathers may be propagated in the same way as the others although it is possible to split up the plants after they have finished flowering. I understand that this method is regarded as rather unprofessional!

PLANTS REFERRED TO IN THIS CHAPTER

AZALEA HYBRIDS

Name	*Type*	*Ultimate height and spread*	*Description*	*Annual rate of growth in author's garden*
Azalea				
Aida	*rustica flore pleno* hybrid	6ft. × 6ft.	Double rose, May/June.	Shoots from base up to 12in.
Alice	Malvatica x *kaempferi* hybrid	4ft. × 4ft.	Pink, May. Good pot plant.	
Anny	,,	4ft. × 4ft.	Orange-red, May. Good pot plant.	
coccinea speciosa	Ghent hybrid	6ft. × 6ft.	Brilliant orange, June. One of the latest to flower.	Shoots from base up to 12in.
Daimio	*kaempferi*	3ft. × 2ft.	Pale orange flowers, late May/June.	3in.
daviesii	Ghent hybrid	6ft. × 6ft.	Creamy-white flowers in June. Fragrant.	Shoots from base up to 12in.
Exbury hybrids		6ft. × 6ft.	All colours from cream to dark red. Large flowers, vigorous. Not so wind-resistant as the smaller-flowered types.	Shoots from base up to 24in.

Name	*Type*	*Ultimate height and spread*	*Description*	*Annual rate of growth in author's garden*
Exquisita	*occidentale* hybrid	6ft. × 6ft.	Cream, flushed pink, wonderful perfume. June.	Shoots from base up to 12in.
Fanny	Ghent hybrid	6ft. × 6ft.	Magenta-pink, June.	Shoots from base up to 12in.
Freya	*rustica flore pleno* hybrid	6ft. × 6ft.	Double salmon-orange. June.	Shoots from base up to 12in.
Gog	Knap Hill hybrid	6ft. × 6ft.	Fine orange, good autumn tints.	Shoots from base up to 18in.
Golden Oriole	,,	6ft. × 6ft.	Golden-yellow, early and vigorous. Sweetly scented.	Shoots from base up to 18in.
Harvest Moon	,,	6ft. × 6ft.	Pale yellow, June.	Shoots from base up to 18in.
Hinodegiri	Kurume hybrid	3ft. × 4ft.	Crimson. Good pot plant.	
Hinomayo	,,	3ft. × 4ft.	Clear pink. Good pot plant.	
Irene Koster	*occidentale* hybrid	6ft. × 6ft.	Rose-pink, late. Delightful scent.	Shoots from base up to 18in.
John Cairns	Malvatica x *kaempferi* hybrid	4ft. × 4ft.	Dark orange-red. Good pot plant.	
Kathleen	,,	4ft. × 4ft.	Deep rose. Good pot plant.	
Knap Hill Yellow	Knap Hill hybrid	6ft. × 6ft.	Clear shade of yellow.	Shoots from base up to 12in.
narcissiflora	Ghent hybrid	6ft. × 6ft.	Double pale yellow.	Shoots from base up to 12in.
Norma	*rustica flore pleno* hybrid	6ft. × 6ft.	Double bright rose. An outstanding colour.	Shoots from base up to 12in.
Orange Beauty	Kurume x *kaempferi* hybrid	4ft. × 4ft.	Magnificent pot plant. Salmon-orange.	
Palestrina	Vuykiana hybrid	4ft. × 5ft.	Pure white flowers. Magnificent pot plant.	
Persil	Knap Hill hybrid	6ft. × 6ft.	White, yellow flare. Late May/June.	,,

Name	*Type*	*Ultimate height and spread*	*Description*	*Annual rate of growth in author's garden*
Phoebe	*rustica flore pleno* hybrid	6ft. × 6ft.	Double sulphur-yellow. May/June.	Shoots from base up to 12in. for both of these.
Satan	Knap Hill hybrid	6ft. × 6ft.	An outstanding scarlet which is *early*.	

RHODODENDRONS

Rhododendron	*Origin of species*			
augustinii	China	6ft. × 6ft.	Mauve to deep blue flowers, May. Lovely.	
Bluebird		3ft. × 3ft.	Pale blue flowers, May.	3–6in.
Blue Diamond		3ft. × 3ft.	Mauve-blue flowers, May.	3–6in.
Blue Tit		Up to 5ft. × 5ft.	Lilac-blue flowers, May.	3–6in.
campylocarpum	Himalaya	6ft. × 6ft.	Magnificent yellow flowers, May.	1–2in.
Carmen		prostrate	Waxy crimson flowers, May.	4–6in.
Countess of Athlone		10ft. × 10ft.	Mauve frilled flowers, late May/June.	6in.
Cynthia		8ft. × 8ft.	Rosy-crimson flowers, late May/June.	6in.
fastigiatum	Yunnan	3ft. × 3ft.	Light mauve flowers, May.	2–3in.
fastuosum flore pleno		10ft. × 10ft.	Double blue-mauve flowers, late May/June.	6–9in.
Gomer Waterer		10ft. × 10ft.	White flowers, tinted blush, May/June.	6–9in.
haematodes	Yunnan	4ft. × 4ft.	Scarlet-crimson flowers, May. Leaves have russety indumentum on underside.	2–3in.
hanceanum nanum		18in. × 24in.	Pale yellow flowers, April.	1in.
hippophaeoides	Yunnan	5ft. × 4ft.	Lavender flowers, April. Said to like boggy soil.	2–3in.
impeditum	China	18in. × 24in.	Mauve or purplish-blue flowers, May. One of the indispensables.	3–4in.
John Walter		12ft. × 12ft.	Rosy-crimson flowers, late May/June.	6–9in.
keleticum	Tibet, Yunnan, Upper Burma	Prostrate	Purplish-crimson flowers, June.	3–4in.

Name	*Origin of species*	*Ultimate height and spread*	*Description*	*Annual rate of growth in author's garden*
Rhododendron				
Lady Chamberlain		Up to 12ft.	A gorgeous shrub. Bell-shaped mandarin red, shading to orange-buff flowers, May/June.	
Lady Clementine Mitford		10ft. × 10ft.	Peach-pink flowers, late May/June.	6–9in.
luteum	E. Europe and Asia Minor	8ft. × 8ft.	The sweetly scented 'Honeysuckle' azalea. Flowers yellow. Good autumn colour.	Shoots from base up to 12in.
Madame de Bruin		10ft. × 10ft.	Cerise-red flowers, late May/June.	6–9in.
Mrs A. T. de la Mare		10ft. × 10ft.	White flowers with a green eye, late May/June.	6–9in.
mucronatum	Japan and China	4ft. × 4ft.	White flowers, May. Belongs to Azalea section.	3–4in.
orbiculare	China	5–6ft. × 5ft.	Pink flowers, May. Attractive round leaves.	3in.
pemakoense	Tibet	6–9in. high spreading habit	Pinkish-purple flowers, April.	
praecox		3–4ft. × 4ft.	Rosy-purple flowers, April/May.	3in.
Purple Splendour		6ft. × 6ft.	Deep purple flowers, late May/June.	6in.
quinquefolium	Japan	8–12ft. × 6ft.	White or pinkish flowers, April/May. Lovely foliage.	
racemosum	China	3ft. × 3ft.	Pink flowers, April/May.	6in.
reticulatum	Japan	6ft. × 6ft.	Purple-mauve flowers, April/May. Lovely foliage.	
russatum	Yunnan	3ft. × 3ft.	Violet-purple flowers, April/May.	3–4in.
schlippenbachii	Japan, Korea	6ft. × 6ft.	Pale pink flowers, April/May. Lovely foliage.	4–6in.
scintillans	Yunnan	3ft. × 3ft.	Lavender to purplish-blue flowers, April/May.	6–9in.
thomsonii	Himalaya	10ft. × 10ft.	Blood-red flowers, May. Glaucous blue-green foliage. Rounded leaves.	
vaseyi	E. North America	8ft. × 8ft.	Pale pink flowers in May. Belongs to the Azalea section of the genus.	4–6in.

Name	*Origin of species*	*Ultimate height and spread*	*Description*	*Annual rate of growth in author's garden*
Rhododendron viscosum	E. North America	6ft. × 6ft.	White or pink fragrant flowers, July. The Swamp Honeysuckle, it belongs to the Azalea section.	6–9in.
williamsianum	China	4ft. × 4ft.	Clear shell pink flowers, April. Lovely rounded leaves.	
yunnanense	China Burma, Tibet	10ft. × 6ft.	White or pink flowers, May.	12–24in.

HEATHS AND HEATHERS

Name	*Origin of species*	*Ultimate height and spread*	*Description*	*Annual rate of growth in author's garden*
Calluna vulgaris alba aurea		6in. × 12in.	Yellow tipped young foliage, white flowers, August/September. Peat.	3–6in.
alba plena		12in. × 18in.	Fine double white, green foliage; white flowers, August/September. Peat.	,,
cuprea		12in. × 18in.	Copper foliage; mauve flowers, late August/September. Peat.	,,
H. E. Beale		24in. × 24in.	Outstanding double rose flowers, September/October. Fine for cutting. Peat.	9–12in.
J. H. Hamilton		9in. × 12in.	Good early double pink. Prostrate growth. August/September. Peat.	3–4in.
Mrs Pat		9in. × 12in.	Intriguing pink tipped foliage; light purple flowers, September/October. Peat.	2–3in.
searlei aurea		18in. × 18in.	Golden foliage, white flowers. August/September. Peat.	6–9in.
Silver Queen		12in. × 18in.	Lovely silver foliage and mauve flowers, September/October. Peat.	3–6in.
Spitfire		9in. × 18in.	Golden foliage with mauve flowers, August/September. A lovely variety. Peat.	,,

Name	*Ultimate height and spread*	*Description*	*Annual rate of growth in author's garden*
Erica arborea alpina	6ft. × 6ft.	Bright green foliage throughout the year. White rather insignificant flowers in spring. Peat.	18in.
carnea aurea	6in. × 18in.	Golden foliage, pink flowers, December/ March.	1–3in.
King George	6in. × 18in.	Rich pink flowers December/March. One of my favourites.	,,
Springwood	6in.	White flowers, December/ March. The best carpeter. Roots as it runs.	3–6in.
Springwood Pink	6in.	Pink flowers, December/ March. Another fine variety for ground cover.	,,
vivellii	6in × 18in.	Dark bronze foliage and carmine flowers. Always the last to bloom but one of the most attractive.	1–3in.
Winter Beauty	6in. × 18in.	Bright pink flowers, December/March.	,,
cinerea C. D. Eason	9in. × 18in.	Dark green foliage, glowing pink flowers. Peat.	3–9in.
Eden Valley	6in. × 15in.	Light green foliage; flowers soft lilac and white, June/August. Peat.	,,
Golden Drop	4in. × 12in.	Golden foliage, prostrate habit; flowers pink, June/August. Peat.	,,
Golden Hue	12in. × 15in.	Bright golden foliage, pale pink flowers, June/ August. Peat.	,,
Lilacina	12in. × 18in.	Light green foliage, pale lilac flowers, June/ August. Peat.	,,
P. S. Patrick	12in. × 18in.	Wine-purple flowers, June/August. Peat.	,,
darleyensis	18in. × 18in.	Pale pink flowers, December/March.	6–9in.

Name	*Ultimate height and spread*	*Description*	*Annual rate of growth in author's garden*
Arthur Johnson	18in. × 18in.	Deeper pink flowers than *darleyensis*, December/March.	6–9in.
George Rendall	9in. × 18in.	An improved form of *darleyensis*, December/March.	„
H. Maxwell	12in. × 12in.	Pink flowers, June/September.	„
Silberschmelze	18in. × 18in.	White flowers, December/March.	„
mediterranea	3ft. × 3ft.	Dark green foliage and pink flowers, March/May.	6–12in.
tetralix Con. Underwood	12in. × 12in.	Crimson flowers, silvery foliage, June/October.	„
vagans Lyonesse	18in. × 24in.	White flowers August/September. Peat.	6–9in.
Mrs D. F. Maxwell	18in. × 24in.	Dark green foliage and deep rose-pink flowers. One of the most beautiful. August/September. Peat.	„
St Keverne	18in. × 24in.	Bright salmon-pink flowers, August/September. Peat.	„

CHAPTER SIX

The Birds, the Bees and the Garden

O Blackbird! sing me something well:
While all the neighbours shoot thee round,
I keep smooth plats of fruitful ground,
Where thou may'st warble, eat and dwell.

Tennyson

No lover of the countryside can ignore its wild inhabitants, and, indeed, their antics provide unfailing interest all the year round. During the winter months we find ourselves quite apprehensive on their behalf, throwing out food and making sure that they will be back in full force to pester us the following spring and summer.

Subconsciously, as we watch the birds fly down for the scraps from our table and observe their uneasy glances, every few seconds, from left to right, we realise how much better is our lot. Danger may surround us everywhere, but we are not watching, as they are, every moment of our lives for the unseen enemy to swoop down and annihilate us. The loss of a leg or of a wing, and they face insuperable odds against survival. This is Nature, stark and relentless.

I have always been interested in birds and the wild life of the countryside. My father, who could recognise most bird songs, taught me a lot on country walks. It was in this way that I gained my earliest experience in the realm of birds. One day, while walking in a country lane, I picked up an unfeathered nestling and took it home. To the astonishment of the family, after being fed with bread and milk for several weeks, it turned out to be a lovely little hen greenfinch. This small bird became extremely tame and used to go about the house with me, perched on my finger. I remember that she was very fond of hemp seeds and as a special treat I used to take her into the pantry to have a good feed of them.

Now in those days, before wild birds were protected by law, you could go into a pet shop and buy a wild bird for as little as sixpence. As I had become so fond of my small finch, my father suggested that I buy her a mate. This I did, and father built a huge cage for the happy pair.

I say 'happy pair' but the male, obviously unused to captivity, was restless and aggressive, and weeks elapsed before he settled down to married life.

The following spring, the little hen showed signs of wanting to build a nest, so strands of an old blanket were pushed through the bars of the cage. These were taken from my fingers and, at close quarters, I watched the nursery being prepared. One by one she laid her five eggs of blotched and mottled grey, lovingly incubating them until the chicks were hatched. She was then allowed into the garden, so that she would have a chance of finding them some natural food, but in vain, one by one they died. Not wanting this to happen again, I released both parent birds and I often wondered what became of them.

House martins used to nest under the eaves of our present house until the wretched house sparrows turned them all out. As soon as they could squeeze into the hole at the top of the nest, the marauders worked away, killing the nestlings by pecking off their heads and throwing them overboard. This done, they then took possession for the raising of their never-ending broods.

I remember seeing a fully-feathered young house martin on the ground beneath one of these nests under the eaves. I picked up the small bird, thinking I would get my husband to put it back when he came home. Ugh! Was it imagination, or did I feel a movement in the feathers near the palm of my hand? Taking no chances, I dropped the poor little thing like a hot brick, and, just in time, for, as it reached the ground, there was a scuffling among its feathers, and, to my astonished and horrified gaze the heads of three huge, sand-coloured creatures revealed themselves to the light. I raced back to the house at the double, emerging with a large carton of a well-known brand of insect powder, liberally peppering it on to the plumage of my nestling. No more monsters appeared so, putting a specimen into a jam jar to back up my tale, I proceeded to put the bird into a box lined with white cloth. Then came a further shock. On to the cloth dropped masses of small red mites so that when my husband did finally appear, he was loth to touch the house martin and had to be forced up the ladder almost at gun point.

One year we found a wren's nest which had been woven into a climbing rose tree that was growing against a pergola post. As the rose tree produced its new shoots, it had squeezed the nest against the support and we found it, too late, full of dead young.

Every March I wait expectantly for the cadence of the willow warbler's song as this, for me, makes spring complete. Every year these tiny migrants nest on the ground in our garden. Every year we try to locate the nests before the magpies detect the parents feeding the young, as once they succeed in doing this they swallow the nestlings like pellets. On two occasions I have actually seen them at work. When we find the nests we cover them with coarse wire netting, through which the willow warblers come and go quite happily. But one year an accident befell one of the parents just as the young had hatched. My husband found five chicks cold and nearly stiff. What should we do? We deliberated upon whether we should leave them any longer, in the hope that the other parent would attend to them, but he, we presumed it was the father, seemed oblivious of the tragedy and could be heard singing in the birch trees.

Willow warblers rarely desert their nests; none of ours had ever done so and a difficult decision faced us. Finally we brought the small birds into the house. It seemed to be the choice of that or certain death. An incubator was hastily rigged up, night light, flower pot, packing and box. Local boys were detailed to scout round for caterpillars, as there did not seem to be a sign of one in the garden! Those brought back were so large and hairy that we realised that we should have to think again. Suddenly it occurred to me to wonder what the parent birds were finding in the birch trees. Armed with a large tin tray and a wooden spoon, I sallied forth to bang the branches. Down they came, aphides by the thousand. My hair, my clothes, were crawling, but the day was saved. Not only were there plenty for the chicks, but almost enough for us too!

Every night the small birds were taken upstairs, put by the bedside, eggcupful of aphides as well, for the first morning feed at the crack of dawn. All went well until the eighth day, when the poor little things developed rickets. They died within a few hours of each other, just as it seemed we were on the brink of success. We knew there was some dietary deficiency, and now realise that had we gone to a pet shop for some vitamins that budgerigar breeders use, we might possibly have saved them.

The favourite resident birds are the hedge sparrows. Inoffensive, undemanding and peaceful, they sing their scratchy little ditty for one's private ear alone. None of this shouting from the house tops for them. One year, a pair bred a cuckoo. The commotion in the garden was so terrific that I hurried out of the house expecting to see a chicken being decapitated by a fox. Instead, sitting on a fence, was a large baby cuckoo, its huge scarlet gape being replenished by a tail-less hedge sparrow. The reason for the lack of tail soon became obvious. As soon as the poor foster-parent turned about to fly off in search of more food, the cuckoo took a savage peck at its retreating form.

An enormous amount of bird-nesting activity begins in my part of Yorkshire during the spring. There was a hedge sparrow's nest in our front hedge which, I remember, attracted nearly all the children from the nearest village. Another year we had a blackbird's nest in this same hedge. We were going on holiday, and as all located birds' nests are usually completely destroyed, we wondered what to do for the best. At last, we had the bright idea of asking one of the local boys to keep an eye on it while we were away, offering him the princely sum of one shilling reward if it was undamaged on our return home. The lad duly took up his position every day after school and I shall never forget our amusement when he came for his pay, followed by a string of smaller satellites, who had obviously been acting as deputies in his absence!

Some of the birds in the garden are extremely tame. Last year we had a missel thrush which nested on the top of the pergola, just opposite the back door. It was a most strategic position, and we gained great amusement from the fact that one of the parents left the nest as soon as any food was thrown out on to the lawn, whereas the other one always waited until the door was firmly shut, before descending to the feast. We were surprised that such a nesting site had been chosen in the first place. Missel thrushes are, as a rule, exceedingly shy birds, and will often desert a nest if they see you even looking in its direction.

What a pest birds can be though! The blackbirds in their dozens, that sit waiting for the fruit to ripen. One can go down the garden and see one looking at a laden gooseberry bush and think to oneself, 'If I don't pick those gooseberries soon, they will be gone. I'll do that after I've watered the plants in the greenhouse.' Alas, when you return, past the gooseberry bush, there sits the blackbird, sated and almost a'hiccup. 'See', he seems to say, staring you straight in the eye, 'I've beaten you to it. I knew I could, even if I bust.'

When one makes a pond, it is little short of a miracle how word gets round the countryside. The first visible tenants are the frogs. In the spring small nostrils emerge from the surface of the water, and a sort of snoring noise is heard. Step closer. There you will see these small creatures wrapped in affectionate embrace. Look again. They have not all survived the hazards of the winter. Here and there in the black mud at the bottom of the pond, bluish-white bellies distended and upturned, are the bodies of the less fortunate. But the lovers croak on, oblivious of death, aware only of the new life they are creating. Later the spawn hatches and the tadpoles emerge. Many of them are consumed by the fish, others by the deadly larvae of the giant water beetle, but still enough survive to blacken the water. It is a better plan to remove the spawn before the tadpoles emerge from the protective jelly, so away it goes by the bucketful to the stream. Here some of it catches in the twigs in the more sluggish reaches, while the rest is borne away by the current.

Newts glide slowly through the water weeds as if stalking a prey. They arrive at the pond in fewer numbers than the frogs and the toads, overland. I had read about this happening without thinking much about it until the day we found a hibernating pair beneath a concrete path we were taking up. And yet I have never seen a newt crossing from pond to pond in the daylight hours. Water boatmen, small water beetles, and a multitude of other insects, combine to make a thriving community, as if the whole of nature is waiting to extend its living room.

I have always been rather a coward about stinging insects, ever since as a child I put my foot into a wasp's nest. When in the garden many years ago, I heard a distant humming. As it grew louder and louder I looked round for the source. Suddenly I became aware of a black cloud advancing in the direction of the house. Now bees are gardeners' friends just so long as they remain working from their hives or, in the case of wild ones, mind their own business, but this was a swarm, and an emergency! Rushing upstairs to close all the windows of the house, I glanced out to see where my husband was. There he stood, immobile, outside the back door, with a sixth sense of impending danger. 'Look out,' I screamed, waving an agitated hand in the direction of the black cloud, 'Take cover.' 'What do you mean, take cover?' he replied, ignoring my frenzied gesture. There was no time to argue and as I hurried downstairs after closing the final bedroom window, I was relieved to hear the sound of the back door closing. We were just in time. The swarm settled on the ground no more than a few yards from the house, and was collected by the local apiarist the next day.

The most amazing good fortune I have ever had was to see a toad eating bees. There he sat, warts and all, phlegmatic and seemingly unseeing at the foot of a dwarf Michaelmas daisy plant in full flower. It was covered with hive bees, and our toad, without a solitary movement other than the flick of his long sticky tongue, swallowed at least twenty of the insects within the space of a few minutes. The bees sensed danger and settled further from the enemy who, after several productive leaps, decided he had appeased his appetite.

I suppose there are wasps' nests in every garden at some time or another and we all rush to destroy them. On the other hand, I had not realised that wasps had a useful purpose until one day, strolling past the vegetable garden, I saw one of these insects buzz past carrying what appeared to be a large lump of green stuff. Curious, I hung about for a few minutes to see whether I could find out what it was doing. Shortly, it came back to a row of cabbages. I followed and was astonished, to say the least of it, when I saw it pick up the remaining half of a good-sized caterpillar, which it had obviously divided for ease of removal. It was no surprise, therefore, when one day a wasp flew through the open door, while I was chopping some meat for a pie, picked a piece up and calmly flew out again.

There are few gardens near pasture land where moles are not troublesome at one time or another. Our moles used to be reasonably well behaved, staying at the bottom of the garden near the stream, until my husband constructed a retaining wall for a peat bed for my choicest plants. Difficulties have resulted of which I had never dreamed.

First of all this nice friable bed seems to be the meeting place for all the local cats. Each morning I find an eruption of paw marks, small hills and valleys, quite attractive if you are not trying to grow plants. Then, just beneath the surface of the soil, the moles have found a perfect feeding ground, seemingly spending the better part of their lives hurrying up and down for their worms and from side to side. Consequently all my small treasures are either buried or exhumed nightly, and one of my first morning jobs is to dash across the garden to assess the damage. Smoke bombs, beer bottles sunk in the ground with necks protruding, every deterrent device has been tried, but the moles continue to regard this patch of soil as their happy hunting ground. They seem to pop up everywhere too. One even appeared through a planting hole in the sun parlour floor. True to form, I was at a loss, knowing that the mole was too short-sighted to be able to see to go out if I opened the door for it, and that if I picked it up it would bite me. My sister, made of sterner stuff, grabbed the small creature and put it outside, but not before it had nipped her finger. And then, of course, I realised that we had actually caught one!

But all the visitors to the garden are not rogues. We found a hedgehog which was running about with its eyes closed. We bathed them and gave the little animal milk for several days but eventually it disappeared and later I found it dead on the road.

It seems to me that if you try to save one thing in the garden you often lose another. We used to net our strawberries until we found that we were enmeshing baby hedgehogs and blackbirds. Finally we thought it better to get rid of the soft fruit so that we could enjoy friends and enemies alike.

Visitors are sometimes quite scathing about our orchard, which is extremely neglected and overgrown. As the rest of the garden is reasonably tidy, this may not make sense, but we have our reasons.

In low-lying situations such as this, it is not much good banking upon a regular fruit crop. Plums do not find the climate much to their liking anyway, often being blighted by keen winds as well as frost. Pears and apples are a little more reliable, but when we first came here, it was doubtful whether we got a fruit crop more than once in seven years. Now some protective willow trees have grown up, and we seem to do a little better, but have lost interest in the general maintenance of the trees.

In our youthful enthusiasm, we used to spray and prune them regularly and I well remember one winter's day when my husband and I set forth, clad from top to toe in protective clothing, with stirrup pump and bucketful of wash.

It is a fact that when a job of this kind is being shared, there is always some confusion as to who is doing the harder part. I started pumping, while the rest of the team sprayed. Tired of the arm-lifting operation involved, my husband thought it would be much easier to pump, so we changed over. After a few strokes at the pump, my partner thought that it was, after all, easier to spray so, wishing to terminate the whole operation in the minimum of time, he started pumping so furiously that the pressure wrenched off the head of the spray from the hose, and I was completely drenched by the viscous yellow fluid. Rather annoyed at being out-manoeuvred, I slunk upstairs to the bath, vowing never to become involved in such a job again, and muttering to myself that if the maggots got the apples, then they at least fed the birds, and, as far as I was concerned, were quite welcome!

CHAPTER SEVEN

The Rock Garden

Each flower and blossom shy
Lingering the live-long day in still delight
Yet without touch of pride,—
J. H. Newman

Rock gardens, like herbaceous borders (not to be confused with mixed borders in which herbaceous plants, annuals, biennials, bulbous plants and shrubs are grown together), seem to be going out of fashion, and certainly this is understandable to me as I have always thought them the most difficult parts of the garden to work. I have been highly critical, too, of the incongruous effects achieved by bringing huge slabs of limestone into small gardens, especially in districts where the local rock is probably sandstone. Nowadays, people are inclined to take their rock gardening less seriously from a constructional point of view, aiming at more natural effects which will display the plants to better advantage. In some ways I am glad to see this happening, as it used to be an all-too-common sight in the North to see front gardens full of chalk-white stones standing on their ends, with not a plant in sight.

Many rock plants are ideal for use in town and suburban gardens, where they can be used as edgings to paths and borders, for ground cover, and even in window boxes. For the enthusiast, the choicest of them can either be grown in troughs or in a cold greenhouse, where their full beauty may be enjoyed at eye level.

I shall not attempt to make a list of the many plants available but rather, as I have tried to do throughout the book, pick out some of the ones that I find attractive and not too difficult from a cultural standpoint.

I am always amazed that the average garden owner seems to know of no other rock plant by name than the Purple Rock Cress or aubrieta. Now the aubrieta, beautiful as it is in flower, has to be clipped over after flowering if it is to remain tidy. It is not, either, the easiest of plants to root from cuttings, so that if you covet a particular colour of it in your neighbour's garden, and he is generous enough to give you a few cuttings, nine times out of ten they die on you, as the saying goes.

Most people do not know, or overlook the sterling merit of the rock roses and rock phloxes. These are both quite easy to root from cuttings, and, if you grow these small phloxes on the edge of a brick or concrete path, you will find an absolute mat of roots developing, ready to be split up into fresh plants. You will be charmed by any of the *Phlox douglasii* or *subulata* sections; Violet Queen is a particular favourite of mine. You may clip or you may neglect to clip these over after flowering. If you do forget, they do not mind very much, and then if they straggle, you often find that they have rooted as they have run.

While I am discussing rock phloxes let me tell you a secret. The experts say that *P. adsurgens* is a difficult plant to grow. It certainly is a lovely one—salmon-pink with a darker stripe in the centre of each petal. Years ago I sent a small order, in which this was included, to a well-known firm. This 'rarity', when it arrived, was unpacked with bated breath. It was beautifully enclosed in a nest of damp green moss. I lowered it lovingly into a well-prepared hole containing soil and peat carefully mixed. Gently firming it in and muttering, 'I've done my best for you, now you do yours', I went on my way.

It is a habit of mine to visit my plants daily, unless anything more urgent deters me, so I stood and stared day after day, hardly believing my eyes when this phlox appeared to be growing. Ten years later I can report that indeed it loves me, even to the extent of producing large numbers of seedlings for my delectation. I have now got several small colonies going and find that the ones that do best for me are in a moist, peaty border facing north.

The rock roses or helianthemums look wonderful growing *en masse*, and will flourish as long as they have sun and reasonably light soil. The individual flowers are short-lived, but do not be put off by this. The colours are all those of the azaleas and indeed, here in the North, I often underplant azaleas with them. As they get older the plants are inclined to straggle unless clipped over in the spring and in a severe winter you will find that some of the wood often dies back.

Single helianthemums seed themselves freely and, once you have them in the garden, will keep themselves going. To keep up supplies of the double varieties, however, it is as well to take cuttings, as, of course, these do not seed themselves. The best time to do this is at the beginning of July, using non-flowering shoots about 3 inches long.

The genus *Saxifraga* is a large one and contains many easy and many difficult plants. Now if you have a large garden that you are trying to

Clematis montana rubens, which grows well in industrial areas

The black-centred, golden flowers of *Rudbeckia speciosa* are produced from August to October

A view of the rock bank which divides the author's garden

Campanula persicifolia does well in shade and looks its best in the middle of a border

maintain without outside help, the word difficult tends to make you shy off, and it is only of late years that I have dared to try a few of the less frequently planted saxifrages.

Saxifraga umbrosa, or London Pride, is a common and useful species, often seen edging paths and being admirably fitted for this purpose. As it seemed difficult to place here, I got rid of it, but I do grow the smaller edition in the form of *S. u. primuloides* Ingwersen's Variety, which makes large mats of pretty miniature rosettes, topped off with 6-inch flower stems.

Saxifrages of the Mossy types irritate a person of my temperament, as I soon lose interest in a plant that needs a lot of attention or, as in this case, one that cannot take care of itself without going bald in the middle. Many people, though, are very fond of the mossy saxifrages, which have a colour range from white to deep crimson. All of these prefer partial shade and a cool root run.

But the ones to which I really want to introduce readers are the less common kinds, those which grow more slowly; admirable plants for, say, a trough or a raised bed where you can see and enjoy in close up the colour, beauty and form of their early flowers. There is a beautiful pink variety called Cranbourne, which you will find in the catalogues in the section labelled 'Kabschia and similar types'. There is a species with primrose flowers named *S. apiculata* that shows its flower heads as early as February among tussocks of bright green. There is Gold Dust of a deeper hue; Faldonside, with citron yellow flowers rising from crimson stems; and *jenkinsae*, a free-flowering pink.

Among the nurseryman's 'Saxifraga, various' you will find listed *S. oppositifolia splendens*, a magnificent purplish-red, flowering in early spring on stems only 1 inch high. This is not such a neat variety as the others I have mentioned, but it is always much admired.

All of these are delightful wee plants and seem to be growing happily in full exposure, with a rooting medium of sandy loam.

The Houseleeks or sempervivums are not everyone's choice, but I would suggest using them on the edges of paths, on dry walls, in troughs, and so on where they soften straight lines. They are evergreen and I like them all. They come in the most subtle shades of red, amber, bronzy-green, wine and variations of green and silver. Some are cobwebbed, some are tipped with red, and when you have a large clump of them the patterns of the rosettes are always attractive. I recently saw a sempervivum I liked called Lady Kelly, but do not ask me where it can be obtained because I would like to know that myself. It had translucent amber foliage, edged with a warmer reddish shading.

When I was first married I was given a pan of the Cobweb Houseleek, *Sempervivum arachnoideum*, which I have never disturbed. It was at least 25 years old then, so that it has adapted itself to living in this same pot for nearly 50 years. It was a gift from an old friend who has since died and I hope that, in time, I myself will be able to pass it down. I doubt very much whether there are any other plants that could put up such a performance with so little attention. Many people admire the flowers of the houseleeks but I consider they detract from the appearance of the plants.

The viola family is large and well known, but I shall comment on two of its members that require less attention than most. These are *Viola gracilis major* and *V. cornuta*. The most endearing of their virtues is that they do not stare at you reproachfully asking to be dead-headed every time you pass their way. These species go on flowering right through the summer months, their blooms never diminishing in size, asking for nothing more than a position which is not too dry. Add to that their sweet perfume and you have two almost perfect plants. *V. cornuta* comes in shades of white, mauve and purple and *V. gracilis* in white, yellow, violet and deep purple.

I am not alone, I am sure, in my admiration of the Madwort, or *Alyssum saxatile*. What a bright patch of gold this makes for us in the spring. Its one fault is that, with age, its growth becomes lanky, but I understand that there is a more compact form called *A. s. compactum*. If you are attracted by paler forms, as I am, you may like to try *A. s. citrinum*. Then there is a biscuity shade, *A. s.* Dudley Neville, but although colour breaks are always exciting to the plant breeder, I can find no enthusiasm for this particular hybrid. A rather different looking plant is *A. spinosum* and its variety *roseum*. These both make dense grey bushes with spines, as the name would suggest.

Many of the Rock Jasmines (androsaces) are considered plants for the expert and many of them are best grown under glass as they dislike winter dampness. However, *Androsace sarmentosa* is among the easiest of them, running about like a strawberry, each runner producing roots and settling down some distance from the parent plant. Some day I should like to start a collection of androsaces as they are great favourites of mine.

Bulbinella hookeri is an uncommon little plant but, for all that, it is perfectly hardy. It throws up in June orangy-yellow flower heads rather like a small Red-hot Poker, except that they are shaped like picture postcard Christmas trees. As Red-hot Pokers suitable for the rock garden are not too hardy in my part of the country, I feel that I can at least achieve the same effect in form. I was surprised to find that *B. hookeri* is related to that rather choice plant, the St Bernard's Lily (*Anthericum liliago*), which is also perfectly hardy.

If you have a suitable position—fairly moist and shady, but well drained—and want to catch out some of your friends, plant a Shooting Star, or *Dodecatheon meadia*. This never fails to stun the natives, with its small reflexed flowers of magenta-pink, with protuberant pointed golden eyes.

For a sunny spot there can be no better plant than *Geranium cinereum subcaulescens*. This covers itself with large magenta-pink, black-eyed flowers all through the summer months. It may not be long-lived; I lost my first plant in a severe winter, but if the parent does die it usually leaves a crop of self-sown seedlings for your future pleasure.

Everyone knows the polyanthus type of primrose, or *Primula*, but not many people are aware that there is a very special variety with reddish-bronze foliage with the tongue-twisting name of *P.* Garryarde Guinevere, bearing pink flowers, which form an absolutely perfect colour association with the leaves. This is as much a favourite with me as the charming variety Wanda and the blue and double varieties of this easy-to-grow section of the primula family, Vernales. Divide them regularly, particularly the double forms, try to find them cool, moist conditions and they will reward you handsomely.

Some town dwellers complain that all the flowers of their primulas and polyanthus are eaten off by the birds. I do not know the answer to this problem, with which I am also faced. I find that in some years the sparrows destroy all the buds, while in others they let them alone, preferring to concentrate on the shrubs.

Of the Auricula section of the genus *Primula*, my first favourites are the ones with bright yellow flowers with white eyes and the bright blues with white eyes. I have found them easily grown from seed and they are charmers, having a most delightful perfume. Auriculas like a rich porous soil and a place in the sun which is not too dry. Curiously enough, the birds seem to leave the flowers well alone.

There are hundreds of species and varieties of primulas, but many of them like moisture and look much better growing by the waterside.

Some of them are extremely difficult and more fitted to the specialist grower.

We read a great deal about the problems of growing lewisias. As I have been growing them for no more than four years, I am not going to do much boasting, but rather describe the conditions under which they survive here. Planted in a moist, peaty, north-facing bed, they give me two periods of bloom, one in the spring and the other in late summer. So far I have only tried the *cotyledon* hybrids, which range in colour from a most unusual apricot-pink to quite a deep rose. Admittedly the rosettes are not multiplying, but the individual plants are becoming larger and larger in size.

Some of the sedums, or Stonecrops, are nothing but a nuisance in the garden, but there are a few pretty spring-flowering varieties which are worthy of inclusion. One of these is *Sedum spathulifolium purpureum*, which has plum-coloured glaucous foliage and bright yellow flowers, a most effective contrast. This is a plant of extremely neat growth and even if, in some years, it is not over-floriferous, you are sure to take pleasure in the colour of its leaves and the arrangement of the rosettes. The variety Capa Blanca has mealy greyish-white foliage which the sparrows enjoy tossing around and about, but which nearly always roots upon landing.

Towards the end of the summer when the lawns have lost their green freshness and are looking dry, and the flowers are wilting in the herbaceous border, perhaps we gardeners are inclined to lapse into a state of lethargy. The rock garden at this time of the year is often the least inspiring of the garden's features. The aubrietas, rock roses, dianthus, rock phlox and alyssum have long been out of bloom, but there are several small plants for late-summer flowering which do not appear to have caught the public eye. *Astilbe simplicifolia*—one of those astilbes commonly known as spiraeas—is one of these and is a most engaging plant with its attractive foliage. There is a pink form, *A. s. rosea*, which is a slightly taller plant. When catering for the needs of all the astilbe family, remember that they prefer damp shady spots and are happiest by the waterside. Then there are the tiniest ones of all, the *A. crispa* varieties. These are perfectly hardy and have flower heads on stalks no more than 6 inches in height.

Many of the rock garden campanulas flower throughout the summer and autumn months. Their numbers are legion and I cannot begin to describe them individually. The ones I seem to have acquired are the ones with the names I am quite unable to pronounce, *Campanula portenschlagiana* (*C. muralis*) and *C. poscharskyana*! But it is the *C. carpatica* group, which begins flowering in July and August, that I find of the greatest value for autumn effect. There are white, blue and purple-blue varieties of this species. The dainty *C. cochlearifolia* (*C. pusilla*) produces its tiny bells of either blue or white from June to September. The blue variety seems to be hardier than the white, which I do not seem to be able to keep for long.

When I am trying to pronounce frightful tongue-twisters like the first two specific names above, I am reminded of the tale one of my friends tells about somebody who got so fed up with being asked the name of every plant in the garden by people who did not really want to know, that she hit upon the brilliant idea of calling everything 'epiglottis'. It appears that it was some time before she was finally caught out!

Among the Evening Primroses, *Oenothera missouriensis* is a late-flowering plant that is quite magnificent and never fails to astound in the production of its huge, papery, lemon-yellow flowers which remain open during the day. It is often in bloom in October and is quite easy to grow, even if it is rather short-lived. It grows freely from seed so it is not difficult to replace.

From mid-July onwards, *Polygonum affine* Lowndes Variety makes a most cheerful patch of colour. I am thrilled with this plant which is a distinct improvement upon the form Darjeeling Red, and appears to be a vigorous grower. I am told that it is in rather short supply and I can well believe it as it has caught the eye of most people who have seen my garden at that time of the year. Later still, but not nearly as showy, colouring in mid-September and through October, is the more trailing knotweed, *P. vaccinifolium*, just the thing for the edge of a wall, over which it can fall.

Sedum floriferum Weinstephener Gold is, as the name would suggest, a golden-yellow. This makes a marvellous patch of colour in the autumn. The foliage is rather on the same lines as that of *S. spurium*. This latter plant, with pale pink heads of flowers, is useful in those parts of the garden where nothing better will grow. There were wide stretches of it in the garden when we came to our present home and I was always carting away great armfuls of it. It has a deep reddish form named *S. spurium* Schorbusser Blut which mingles well with it and is equally vigorous—but, oh, what a name! They are both plants I can live happily without.

Small Shrubs

No rock garden or bank seems to me to be complete without a few small shrubs, and, of these, who has not succumbed to the charms of the dwarf brooms? They are all good-tempered, if somewhat short-lived, provided they are given a place in the sun.

Genista pilosa is a first-rate prostrate species, ideal for growing over the edge of stones in the rock garden. Given the right conditions of sun and light sandy soil, each spring it will cover itself with masses of golden flowers. If the conditions are not so good, it will do little worse. Here is a plant that withstands dry climates and cold ones and has the endearing habit of rooting as it runs. In general the dwarf brooms are not easy to root from cuttings, but this is one of the exceptions and perhaps this is a good thing too, as my specimens do not appear to set their seed. In time, you may find that *G. pilosa* has outgrown its position but it can always be chopped back to the nearest layering.

Genista sagittalis is that curious broom with the winged branches. It is engaging as a carpeter, producing an evergreen effect, but I have not found it as hardy as *G. pilosa*. The Spanish Gorse, *G. hispanica*, is prickly and makes a fine cushion of yellow in early June. It is one of the species that revels in chalk, which is probably why it does not do so well as it might here. A few pieces of this broom, pulled off with a heel, in July, and put in a pot of sandy soil, will root readily and there you have the ideal Christmas or birthday gift. Remember to present these cuttings in their pots as the plants resent root disturbance.

Genista lydia has slender pendulous shoots, with flowers in clusters along the stems. This is regarded by many people as one of the best of the dwarf brooms and I am sure that you will like it as much as I do. It does not set seed for me and I presume that it is propagated by cuttings.

Genista radiata is another small broom of which I am very fond. It grows to about 3 feet, flowering in June and seeding freely on my rock bank. It is, therefore, of great value, as brooms as a whole cannot be said to be long lived and this is one that can be relied upon to propagate itself. The Dyer's Greenweed, *G. tinctoria flore pleno*, has only recently been added to my collection. The leaves of this plant give it more body than many of the other brooms I have described, in that they sit more closely on the stems and are of a very glossy bright green. Unfortunately it seems prone to attacks by blackfly. It is, however, a pretty broom, with long terminal racemes of flower which appear in high summer.

Cytisus kewensis is, to my eyes, one of the most attractive of all dwarf brooms, producing, early in the spring, an absolute cascade of cream flowers of the same tone as *C. praecox*. These sheets of bloom look wonderful in association with the Rock Jasmine, *Androsace sarmentosa*, which I have mentioned earlier in the chapter (p. 98). *C. kewensis* seldom grows more than 18 inches in height and is a distinct 'must'.

Cytisus nigricans was grown from seed received from Wisley several years ago and I was quite surprised by the result. It is certainly different from the others in appearance, flowering at the tips of its shoots in July and August. Eventually it makes a shrub of 3 feet or more and is a most useful species for late colour.

And so I could go on admiring the dwarf brooms. There are lots more of them, any of which are sure to please.

Dwarf Conifers

The dwarf conifers are such fascinating little evergreens that I can never understand why it is that they are not more widely planted, and, of course, they are perfect in the rock garden for winter effect. The more slowly they grow, the more gnarled they become, so that any worries about growth, in respect of atmospheric pollution, go by the board.

We will begin with a fastigiate 'baby', which is one of the most fascinating of all. This is the Noah's Ark Tree, *Juniperus communis compressa*. This glaucous, blue-grey, miniature Italian Cypress takes years to reach 1 foot in height and is an absolute pet. It is perfectly simple to propagate too. Cuttings taken off with a heel in July, dipped in hormone rooting powder, and placed round the edge of a pot of sandy soil, will, if kept moist and covered with polythene, seldom fail to root by late autumn. Once, having no coarse sand when I required it, I brought up a trugful from the bed of the stream and have found it by far the best rooting medium I have ever struck.

While I am discussing the propagation of dwarf conifers, I think it as well to mention that we are told to take our cuttings from as low down on the plants as we can, as the higher on the plant the cutting, the larger the ultimate specimen is likely to be, if indeed it does not revert to a normal-sized conifer. That this is so I have no doubt, as there are several conifers in the garden that I have bought as being suitable for rock gardens, only to find that they have just grown and grown. In one case, a large gap was left when I removed an enormous juniper, somewhat belatedly, I must admit. These gaps are the ones in front of which visitors invariably pull up sharply, even in the midst of animated, if irrelevant conversation, to say, 'Whatever has happened here! Have you taken something out?' One is then obliged to explain, in something of an apologetic undertone, 'Oh well, the garden is always in a state of flux you know.'

Picea albertiana conica is another of my favourites. It stands up to the atmospheric pollution well for a spruce, even if it does sometimes turn a rather unhealthy green at the end of a dry summer, and gives real pleasure in the symmetry of its emerald pyramid. What it does dislike, in common with all plants, is draughts. In this sort of position it will brown on the exposed side, though not as badly as others of this family. It is simple to propagate and grows at the rate of about 1 inch a year. *P. abies clanbrassiliana* is a bun-shaped spruce of exceptionally slow growth and attractive habit.

Thuja orientalis elegantissima is an upright golden dwarf that I first saw growing in the moist, unpolluted Irish air, and what a lively colour the foliage was there! I liked it at once, obtained a specimen myself and find I am continually admiring its colour and dense globose form. I should say that it is quite my best thuja, immeasurably superior to *T. occidentalis* Rheingold, which is of far looser habit and, with me, has become rather straggly with age.

One of the cedars, *Cedrus libani* Comte de Dijon, was growing well until I moved it into a fresh position. Since it has been moved, although I replanted it carefully, it has looked very sick and will probably die. This is a pity as I was extremely proud of it. The lesson to be learned from this is that expensive little conifers should be put into their permanent positions as soon as they are received from the nursery. The difficulty is that as they grow older their habit often changes, appearing to be quite different from what you had visualised in the first place. This particular specimen developed a rather drooping look and was quite wrong for the original position in which it was planted. I have a suspicion it may have been the weeping form, *C. l. sargentii.*

Tsuga canadensis pendula, as the name implies, is another weeping conifer. This hemlock has foliage like a dainty yew tree but with more variation in the tone, the young growth being of a lighter green and persisting longer than is usual with most evergreens. My specimen is of slow growth and has taken 10 years to reach a foot in height, but I have seen plants of at least 5 or 6 feet in other gardens.

As I had tried the Japanese cedar, *Cryptomeria japonica elegans*, years ago and lost it, I did not think that I should have much luck with this family but, to my amazement, the dwarf *C. j. vilmoriniana* lived through the severe winter of 1962. It is making a bright green, densely globose shrub.

Dwarf Shrubs for Acid Soils

Some of the small rhododendrons, as well as the heathers, are good subjects for the rock garden. All rhododendrons are so easily moved at any age that it does not matter much if you choose one which is eventually too big for the intended position. It always seems a pity to me that people are afraid of ultimate heights. Plants and trees can always be removed when they become overgrown and in an industrial area many vigorous trees and shrubs take a lifetime to become of nuisance value.

Now I am going to mention one or two other dwarf shrubs that are suitable for acid conditions, or neutral soils with the addition of peat.

The Bog Rosemary, *Andromeda polifolia nana*, bears, from May onwards, clusters of bright pink bell-shaped flowers a little larger than heather and, once it becomes established, spreads rapidly by means of underground stems. It likes cool, moist conditions so if there is a drought in your district during the summer months, be sure to keep an eye open to see that it does not dry out. This plant has real charm, is evergreen, perfectly hardy, and does very well for me. There is a white form of it, *A. p. alba.*

Cassiope lycopodioides is another equally fascinating evergreen, sometimes called the Japanese Heath. In this case the creamy-white, bell-shaped flowers are suspended over the plant on stems no thicker than human hair. It is slower in growth than the Bog Rosemary and, if you like it, you may be encouraged to try other species, although these seem to make larger plants. In the hope that they will do well for me I have lately acquired *C.* Edinburgh, *C. fastigiata*, an upright form, and *C. selaginoides*. More delightful small plants could not possibly be found.

The Gromwell, *Lithospermum diffusum* Heavenly Blue, is a wonderful evergreen creeping shrub that I would not like to be unable to grow. This is the one which produces those bright deep blue flowers, almost like Forget-me-nots, in the spring and sporadically throughout the year. Plant it in peaty loam in a fairly moist open position, topdress it with peat annually and, if you keep a sharp eye open in the spring, you may be lucky enough to find some self-sown seedlings lurking in its depths. Pot them up before they get smothered. I had always tried to propagate this plant by pulling off short lateral shoots from the current year's growth, but this is not the best way at all. Tip cuttings, 2 inches in length taken in July, dibbled round the edge of a pot containing a mixture of sand and peat and covered with a polythene bag, should give 100 per cent success. I am always fascinated by the roots of this plant, which are a lovely pink, and would almost beg you to handle them carefully. You may find that a harsh winter will deal unkindly with this most precious of dwarf shrubs, so it is advisable to take cuttings annually. Do remember to keep either seedlings or cuttings under glass the first winter of their lives as, for some unaccountable reason, they die if they are put out into the open garden in the autumn.

Polygala chamaebuxus grandiflora, the Milkwort, is another charming small shrub, with tiny yellow pea-like flowers with purple wings. My plant died in the exceptionally cold winter of 1962, but its replacement, provided by a good friend, has survived so far. It is said to grow to a height of about 6 inches, with a spread of 1 foot, but it is growing slowly here. It is said, also, to prefer peat and leafmould, but I am not altogether convinced that this is so.

Rock Plants from Seed

One of my friends has suggested that I should name some of the easiest rock plants to grow from seed. I have already mentioned rock roses (helianthemums) and one or two others. There are magnificent strains of many rock plants available, including some double forms of aubrieta. I always think aubrietas are better grown from seed than from cuttings, unless a particular variety is required. *Alyssum saxatile*, too, is easy and builds up into more compact plants when grown from seed. For lovers of the Columbine, *Aquilegia alpina* Hensoll Harebell is charming. Seeds of alpine pinks germinate freely and a good stock can readily be built up from such kinds as *Dianthus allwoodii*, *D. alpinus*, *D. deltoides*, *D.* Little Jock and so on. *Thymus serpyllum coccineus* and Pink Chintz are worth attempting, although the colours may be somewhat variable from seed. The easiest of all are the violas. You may like to try *Viola cornuta* and *V. gracilis*. If you like pansies, or *Viola wittrockiana*, the range of colours is bewildering and a packet of mixed seed of a good strain will provide interesting results. I feel here that I should mention a remark passed by another of my friends about these flowers. She said, 'Why on earth don't they tell us that the faces of pansies follow the sun?' Evidently she had planted a row of them in a west-facing border, so that when she went into her garden in the afternoons all the flowers had their backs to her. Planted on the other side of the path they would, of course, have been quite satisfactory, and it is a point worth bearing in mind.

Small bulbs, too, may be raised from seed. This is a cheap method of producing stocks of chionodoxa, crocuses, muscari, scillas and others. In these cases, though, the young bulblets should be left in clearly labelled seed pans for a few years until they have grown to flowering size, for if they are planted out too soon there is a danger that they may be accidentally destroyed when the soil is being forked over.

I find that most of my failures in connection with growing plants from seed are due to carelessness. Many of us sow our seeds carefully in light sandy soil, covering the pan with glass and newspaper until germination takes place. Thinking that the battle is over and victory achieved, we then remove the paper and glass in one fell swoop, often leaving the tender seedlings exposed to bright sunlight. If a little more care could be taken by removing the glass gradually and leaving the seed pan or box in the shade for a few days, the results would probably be more satisfactory.

PLANTS REFERRED TO IN THIS CHAPTER

Name	*Origin of species*	*Height*	*Remarks*
Alyssum			
saxatile	E. Europe	9–12in.	Deep yellow flowers, April/June.
citrinum		9–12in.	Pale yellow flowers, April/June.
compactum		6in.	Deep yellow flowers, April/June.
Dudley Neville		9in.	Biscuit-yellow flowers, April/June.
spinosum	S. Europe	6–8in.	Makes dense spiny bush with small white flowers, May/June.
roseum		,,	Pink flowers.
Andromeda polifolia			
alba		9in.	Delightful shrub spreading by underground runners. Peat loving. Flowers white, May.
nana		9in.	Flowers bright pink.

Name	*Origin of species*	*Height*	*Remarks*
Androsace sarmentosa	Himalaya	2–5in.	Bright rose flowers, May/June, from hairy rosettes.
Anthericum liliago	S. Europe	12–18in.	Spikes of white flowers, June/July.
Aquilegia alpina Hensoll Harebell		12in.	Deep blue or blue and white flowers, May.
Astilbe crispa		6in.	Short spikes of flowers, August. White, pink and rose.
simplicifolia	Japan	6–9in.	Fluffy white flowers, August.
rosea		,,	Pink flowers, August.
Aubrieta	Sicily and Asia Minor	6in.	Cushion-like plants flowering in early spring. Wide range of colours from white to pink and purple.
Bulbinella hookeri	New Zealand	18in.	Orange-yellow spikes, June.
Campanula			
carpatica	Carpathian Mts.	9–18in.	Blue and white flowers, July/August.
cochlearifolia	European Mts.	4–6in.	Blue and white flowers, June/August.
portenschlagiana	S. Europe	6–9in.	Blue and white flowers, June/July.
poscharskyana	Dalmatia	9–12in.	Blue, June/July.
Cassiope			
Edinburgh		10in.	Large white flowers, April/May.
fastigiata	Himalaya	6–10in.	White flowers, April/May.
lycopodioides	N.E. Asia and N.W. America	1–1½in.	White flowers, April/May.
selaginoides	Himalaya and W. China	9in.	White flowers, April/May. All cassiopes are peat loving.
Cedrus libani			
Comte de Dijon		5ft. but grows only a few inches annually	Dwarf form of the Cedar of Lebanon.
sargentii		,,	Weeping form.
Cryptomeria			
japonica vilmoriniana		2½ft.	Dwarf form growing about 1 inch annually.
Cytisus			
kewensis		18in.	Procumbent shrub flowering May/June. Cream.
nigricans	Central and S.E. Europe	3–6ft.	Deep yellow flowers, July and August.
praecox		3–5ft.	Cream flowers, May.
Dianthus			
allwoodii	Europe	4–12in.	White to purplish-pink flowers, summer.

Name	*Origin of species*	*Height*	*Remarks*
Dianthus			
alpinus	Austrian Alps	4in.	Pink to purple flowers, June/August.
deltoides	Europe	6–9in.	Deep pink to purplish-red flowers, June/August.
Little Jock		3–6in.	Pink flowers, May/July.
Dodecatheon meadia	E. North America	1–1½ft.	Purplish-pink flowers, May.
Genista			
lydia	E. and S.E. Europe	24in.	Yellow flowers, June.
hispanica	S.W. Europe	1–2ft.	Spiny shrub with yellow flowers, June.
pilosa	S. Europe	Prostrate shrub from 6–20in.	Yellow flowers, June.
radiata	Central and E. Europe	Shrub of about 3ft.	Golden flowers, June.
sagittalis	Central and S.E. Europe	Prostrate shrub of about 9–12in.	Winged branches. Yellow flowers, June.
tinctoria flore pleno		6in.–2ft.	Yellow flowers, July.
Geranium cinereum subcaulescens		6–9in.	Magenta flowers, June and throughout the summer.
Helianthemum species and varieties		12in.	Rock Roses. Small shrubs flowering in May and June and sporadically throughout the summer. Wide colour range from white to dark red. Single and double flowers.
Juniperus communis compressa		1–2ft.	Slow-growing conifer with upright habit.
Lewisia cotyledon	California	6–12in.	Pinkish-apricot flowers in spring and again in the summer.
Lithospermum diffusum Heavenly Blue		Prostrate shrub of 6–8in.	Striking blue flowers, May onwards. Peat lover.
Oenothera missouriensis	South Central U.S.A.	Sprawling plant of about 6–9in.	Lemon-yellow flowers 3–4 inches across, July onwards.
Phlox			
adsurgens	California	6–12in.	Salmon-pink flowers, May/June onwards.
douglasii	W. North America	2–6in.	Lavender, white and pink flowers, May.
subulata	Eastern U.S.A.	2–6in.	Lavender, white and pink flowers, May.

Name	Origin of species	Height	Remarks
Picea albertiana			
conica		6–8ft.	Slow-growing conifer making about 1 inch of growth annually.
abies clanbrassiliana		6ft.	Slow-growing bun-shaped conifer.
Polygala chamaebuxus grandiflora		6in.	Crimson and yellow pea-like flowers, May/June. This small shrub likes lime.
Polygonum affine Lowndes Variety		6–9in.	Mat forming. Rosy-red flowers, July onwards.
Polygonum vaccinifolium	Himalaya	6–9in.	Bright rose flowers, September/October. Good for a wall.
Primula Garryarde Guinevere		4in.	Pale pinkish-mauve flowers, reddish-bronze leaves.
Wanda		4in.	Deep reddish-purple flowers, early spring.
Saxifraga			
apiculata		3–4in.	Cushion type with primrose flowers, early spring.
Cranbourne		3–4in.	Cushion type with pink flowers, early spring.
Faldonside		3–4in.	Cushion type with yellow flowers, early spring.
Gold Dust		3–4in.	Cushion type with bright yellow flowers, early spring.
jenkinsae		3–4in.	Cushion type with pink flowers, early spring.
oppositifolia splendens		1in.	Intense purplish-red flowers, early spring.
umbrosa	Europe	12–18in.	London Pride. Pink flowers, early summer. Likes shade.
primuloides Ingwersens Variety		6in.	Small version of London Pride.
Sedum floriferum Weinstephener Gold		2in.	Golden-yellow flowers, summer and autumn.
spathulifolium purpureum		3in.	Evergreen plum-coloured foliage, yellow flowers, spring.
Capa Blanca		3in.	Greyish-white foliage and yellow flowers.
spurium	N. Persia	3in.	Pinkish flowers, August/September.
Schorbusser Blut		3in.	Deep red flowers, August/September.
Sempervivum			
arachnoideum	Pyrenees		Cobweb Houseleek.
Lady Kelly			Houseleek with amber rosettes.

Name	*Origin of species*	*Height*	*Remarks*
Thymus serpyllum coccineus	Europe	1–3in. Prostrate	Deep reddish-purple flowers, June/July.
Thuja occidentalis Rheingold		5ft.	Small conifer with golden foliage in summer, bronze in winter.
orientalis elegantissima		9ft.	Upright golden dwarf conifer making about 1–2 inches' growth annually.
Tsuga canadensis pendula		Ultimately makes a bush of 5 to 6ft.	Slow-growing conifer with pendulous branches.
Viola			
cornuta	Pyrenees	4–12in.	White, mauve and purple flowers, throughout summer.
gracilis	Asia Minor Balkan peninsular	4–6in.	White, yellow, violet and deep purple flowers, summer.
major		4–6in.	Deep purple.
wittrockiana		4in.	The garden pansy in all its wonderful colours.

CHAPTER EIGHT

Bulbs and Corms

The little fires that Nature lights—
The scilla's lamp, the daffodil—
Joseph Campbell

The flowers of spring have always been more attractive to me than those of the autumn. They tempt the gardener from the fireside just as they attract the bees from their hives.

The newspapers are always full of reports of rarities flowering unseasonably, but when we find the first spring bulbs in flower in our own gardens, we feel a buoyancy of spirit that can be captured at no other season of the year. We know that the curtains of winter are about to rise so that we may once again see the delights of spring being re-enacted. Small bulbs are the tapestry from which the spring carpet is woven. They seem to ignore the gardener's neglect and some of them increase so rapidly as to become an embarrassment. They are all wonderful, especially when grown *en masse*.

The ones that give me particular pleasure are the crocuses, and I shall begin with these. The earliest are the species and they throw up such multitudes of flowers, each with its own bright orange stigma, that they are almost unbelievably beautiful. If there is no sun to shine on them so early in the year, their full beauty fades before they open. Fortunately this rarely happens, and I can think of nothing more lovely than large clumps of these little treasures opening to the warmth of the spring sunshine and distilling their musky perfume upon the air.

You must plant lots of *C. tomasinianus*, that frail flower that rises like a pale ghost out of the soil and opens to reveal its purple silken lining. The varieties of this species, Barr's Purple, Taplow Ruby and Whitewell Purple, are all desirable, so buy as many of them as you can afford. Try to grow them in groups of one colour and contrast one group with another. For example, the *C. chrysanthus* variety E. A. Bowles would look delightful with one with really blue tones like the popular *C. c.* Blue Pearl, and *C. tomasinianus* Taplow Ruby goes well with the

The spurges are strangely fascinating plants. In the spring *Euphorbia epithymoides* bears 'flowers' of bright yellow

Lenten Roses, *Helleborus orientalis*, in varying shades from greenish-cream to deep purple, flower in February-March

Left : *Lychnis coronaria*, the Rose Campion, is a popular garden plant with crimson-magenta flowers and silver foliage. Right: Another silver-leaved plant is the giant *Onopordon arabicum*, reaching 4 to 5 feet

Stachys lanata is the 'Lamb's Ear', silver-leaved and with pinky-mauve flowers

chrysanthus variety Cream Beauty. Then there is *C. sieberi*, with its lovely variety Violet Queen and so on.

The larger and slightly later-flowering Dutch crocuses are equally splendid in the garden, but do not form such refined mosaics of colour as the species. Again, try not to mix the colours when planting them and do not plant them in rows! The blues and the whites look wonderful together, but I think the orange ones look much better on their own.

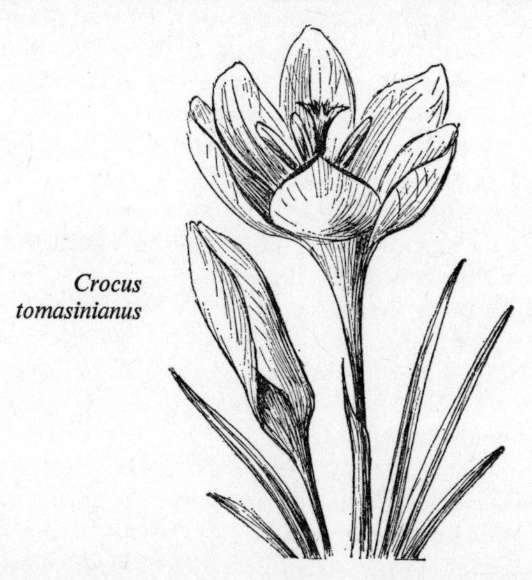

Crocus tomasinianus

If you grow crocuses, beware of mice. They adore the corms and I have seen the tiny creatures, eyes bulging, flanks bursting, eating them in broad daylight. The only traces left of their depredations are the husks on the surface of the soil. When they eat the bulbs in active growth, the cormless stems are either left to wilt in the holes, or are strewn about in improvident profusion. I understand that they do not consume the corms of *C. tomasinianus*. I cannot say that I have any proof of this, but I have noticed that they certainly prefer to eat the yellow-flowered types, particularly of the *chrysanthus* hybrids. Nothing is more heart-rending than to see large colonies of these beautiful spring bulbs completely destroyed by these engaging little creatures—and yet one hesitates to get rid of them.

In the days of our first dog, Lou Lou, I remember hearing an excited yapping in the direction of the rock bank. Arriving breathless, I found a most charming mother-to-be field mouse, hands cupped in supplication, sitting on the rock garden and, opposite, tongue lolling to catch the drops of blood slowly oozing from a nip on the nose, my fearless and trusted hound, too terrified to do more than bark.

Mice do not only like crocuses. I remember buying a hundred yellow tulip bulbs from someone who was leaving the village. As it was too early in the year to plant them, I hung them up in a carrier bag, suspended to a bar in the greenhouse roof and, one would have thought, quite out of reach of anything. When I went to plant them, there was the bag, outwardly looking exactly the same, but containing a collection of husks! I suggested to my husband that he set a trap. 'What, and kill the poor little things? They have lovely white tummies, and you should put your bulbs in a safe place.' Retribution struck fast. A few weeks later all his freshly planted chrysanthemum stools were nibbled off at ground level. Traps were set and five of the little dears, white tummies and all, met an unsentimental end!

My next favourites among the spring bulbs are the chionodoxas, especially in the species *sardensis*. Most of the chionodoxas have flowers of varying shades of blue, with white centres, but the eye of *sardensis* is inconspicuous. Another one of which I am very fond is *Chionodoxa gigantea*. With a larger white eye, *C. luciliae* dazzles in its spring display and the pink form of this, *C. luciliae* Pink Giant, is most attractive. I find these little bulbs more graceful in habit than the scillas. They seed profusely and can be relied upon to multiply rapidly by this means. I cannot have too many of them in the garden. I had long been rather confused about identifying the two families, but I have now learned that chionodoxas have petals which are joined together at the base, whereas the petals of scillas are independent of each other.

The snowdrop, *Galanthus nivalis*, and its variety *flore pleno*, is a 'must' in every garden and I am quite happy with these two kinds. I have tried to establish some of the larger flowered ones, but they do not seem to linger, so I make do with what I have and, for increase, divide them up as soon as they go out of bloom. I find it easier to divide all small bulbs as soon as the flowers go over. The job is then done, the colours can be arranged to best advantage and, in any case, it is better not to leave them out of the ground longer than can be avoided.

If you do not already know them, let me now introduce you to what I think are some of the most beautiful of all spring flowers, but which do not seem to be planted in my part of Yorkshire to any great extent.

These are the erythroniums. *Erythronium dens-canis*, the Dog's-tooth Violet, is the easiest of the family, having dainty pinkish flowers, with reflexed petals, which hover over the marbled leaves of green and mahogany. There are varying shades of pink in its forms, and a white one, which I do not think blends with the foliage as well as the pinks. The yellow-flowered *E. tuolumnense*, is quite a different plant. The leaves are a bright, unspotted lustrous green, and the much smaller flowers are borne on longer stems. To get a good effect with these you have to wait until you have a large clump of them. The variety White Beauty has a most fitting name. The graceful, creamy-white flowers are borne on 6-inch stems, hovering over the glossy, slightly marbled leaves. I understand that there is a pink form of *tuolumnense* although I have not yet acquired it.

If you wish to divide your erythroniums, this must be done immediately after flowering as the foliage soon disappears. All are best in dampish situations.

Even the word 'Violet' brings a shudder to my frame. Years ago I introduced a few plants of the common dog violet here. They looked so pretty growing in the cracks of my brother's crazy paving, that I felt I must copy the idea. It was the worst thing I ever did. Now they are everywhere in their millions. I thought I had read that these plants seeded without flowering, and this would not have surprised me, but my botanist friends tell me that they have insignificant secondary flowers, which seed under cover of darkness, as you may say. The roots of these dog violets grow in thick bunches, out of all proportion to the size of the visible foliage, and are a nightmare in the way in which they infiltrate into the hearts of your choicest plants. Every year, when forking over the garden in the spring, I pull out as many as I can and, every year, a percentage more come up to take their places. So beware, all recipients of my offerings and inexperienced gardeners all, never be charmed into admitting them to the garden.

We are told that the Snake's-head Fritillaries, *Fritillaria meleagris*, are natives of this country, being found growing wild in damp meadows. Although they do not spread quickly for me, they are such gracefully lovely flowers that they cannot be excluded from the spring garden. One cannot help but be entranced by the chequered patterns on their petals or by the subtlety of colour of the plain ones.

This brings me to the Crown Imperial, *F. imperialis*. Now this, with me, is a most aggravating plant, in that it does not die, neither does it flower. I think I have been growing it in various positions for over 20 years, without any success. My brother sent me a box of them from his garden on the edge of the Cotswolds and this, then, must be the secret. They must like lime in the soil. I gave a few bulbs to my friend in the East Riding of Yorkshire and each spring she shows me massive heads of this most noble of plants. As an excuse for the covetousness I feel, I feign indifference, saying, 'Oh well, they smell awful anyway'. Actually I do find the smell of both foliage and bulb pretty ghastly, but I would like to produce a few flowers occasionally! My only consolation is that no one else locally seems to do much better with them.

As my friend also manages to grow the winter aconites, *Eranthis hyemalis*, I have a suspicion that they too may prefer the addition of a little lime to the soil, but they are certainly not suited by the conditions here and just fade out after a year or two, if they come up at all. Looking through my gardening records, I find that I have had no luck with alliums either.

But it is not all failure. The grape hyacinth, *Muscari armeniacum*, is a very obliging small bulb and increases rapidly. Put them where you do not mind seeing the rather untidy foliage, which appears in the autumn and persists until well after the flowers have faded at the end of April. These small bulbs may be left for years undisturbed although, if you have the patience to do it, it is better to divide them up about once every three or four years. The grape hyacinths are in flower at about the same time as the miniature daffodils and look well in association with them. I have recently tried an earlier flowering one, with sky blue bells, named in the bulb catalogues *M. azureum*, and wish I had planted it before. This is really a hyacinth and should be correctly named *Hyacinthus azureus*. The two families are closely allied but the difference may be recognised by the fact that the bells of the hyacinth do not show a constriction at the mouth of the tube as do the muscari. The Feather Hyacinth, *M. comosum monstrosum* refuses to stay with me for more than a year or two and eventually dies out.

The Summer Snowflake, *Leucojum aestivum* Gravetye, does well here. This is a surprising bulb. Flowering in late April or early May, the strong shiny, dark green, daffodil-like leaves thrust their way through the soil until you expect a flower of almost the calibre of a hippeastrum. Not so. On quite a substantial stem hang, in a terminal umbel, several bell-shaped white flowers, scalloped and tipped with green. These are delightful blooms for cutting, but in the garden I never know quite where to put them, although I have seen some good effects achieved by growing the bulbs at the waterside.

The Spring Snowflake, *L. vernum*, is really lovely and I am surprised it is not more popular. It flowers in late February and early March and is not such a robust grower as *L. aestivum*. Planted under a birch tree my bulbs look quite natural and for garden effect I prefer this species. It likes a moisture-retentive soil. Snowflakes can easily be distinguished from snowdrops by the fact that the six segments of the perianth are of equal length, whereas the three inner ones of the snowdrops are con-considerably smaller than the outer ones.

Of the Squills or scillas, *Scilla tubergeniana* is the first, thrusting its pale blue flowers out of the soil in February at the same time as the earliest crocuses. My favourite is *S. bifolia*, dainty and star-like in flower. The lovely *S. sibirica* is the best known squill and I find it perfect in association with the brilliant, many-headed, scarlet dwarf tulip, *Tulipa praestans*. The tulips are growing at the foot of a wall facing west, where they are left completely undisturbed from year to year. With the scillas they provide one of the most striking colour groupings in the spring garden.

I have not had nearly the success with tulips that I have had with narcissi. Many of the Cottage and Darwin varieties will flower well for a few years but, whether lifted or not, seem to lose vigour. This is possibly due to the nature of the soil. Tulips prefer a light sandy loam and a hot dry summer in which the bulbs can be well ripened. In view of this, and fond as I am of them, I feel that they are not the best buy for me. They are essential for town bedding schemes, however, giving long-lasting displays of the most wonderful colour. I consider the Lily-flowered tulips the most lovely, these being the epitome of grace.

Among the species, apart from *T. praestans*, the only ones I have had any luck with are *T. tarda* and *T. biflora* but, even so, I would hesitate to say that these are growing really well. I recently bought some of the *T. greigii* hybrids. The broad leaves of these, heavily marked with broken chocolate-coloured shadings, are most attractive and the brilliantly coloured flowers range from cream to vermilion, many of them having delightfully contrasting centres.

Who can resist the miniature daffodils? And yet how difficult they are to keep in my garden. *Narcissus triandrus albus*, known as Angel's Tears, will have none of me. *N. asturiensis* (*N. minimus*) holds its own but does not increase. *N. bulbocodium*, on the other hand, is reasonably happy and seeds freely. Should the parent bulbs die there are always plenty of young plants to replace them, including some of the paler form, *N. bulbocodium citrinus*, which I find more attractive than the type.

Narcissus cyclamineus is a very poor doer, although it is perhaps the loveliest of them all with its small reflexed flowers of bright gold. By contrast its hybrids February Gold and March Sunshine increase rapidly. Unfortunately the flowers of these two varieties are nearly the same size as the ordinary garden narcissus, a fact which does not always register when one is reading the catalogues, but they do carry a refinement which is absent from the larger types. I was amazed to read of these varieties being in bloom in a southern garden in February. The ones here are always later than Helios, the earliest narcissus to flower in my garden, except for one or two miniatures.

The *N. triandrus* hybrids Tresamble and Thalia do very well. Their dainty heads of several white flowers have a delightfully cool, crystalline appearance, and, when cut, are wonderful for floral arrangements.

Daffodils may be said to thrive on this soil and are planted everywhere. When the first few hundreds were put in I had no idea what they would look like nearly 30 years later. They multiply in their thousands and, of course, as they were planted so long ago, there are many old hybrids that are now considered obsolete.

For naturalising, Helios is the variety which pleases me most, having stood up to the disadvantages of growing in rough grass, often mown before the foliage has died down completely. Helios is a lovely deep yellow self, with a medium trumpet. The sturdy stems are frequently fractured by a continuous series of late spring frosts, so that they may pick themselves up during the day, only to be laid low again during the following night. Sometimes they are flattened to the ground at least a dozen times and, when the stems have grown to about 9 inches or so, it will be readily understood what a strain this must be on the plants. Often it will cause the flower heads to fall over about 4 inches from the neck, but if these faulty blooms are removed at once, the general effect is not spoiled.

The next on my list of good garden daffodils for naturalising is that very old variety Sir Watkin. With this—Sir Watkin is little later flowering than Helios and slightly paler in colour—I have two varieties that have bloomed well for years without attention and that are admirably fitted for growing in rough grass. A few years ago I bought a hundred Sempre Avanti, with bicolored flowers, for the same purpose, but these have not done nearly as well as I had hoped, losing vigour and increasing slowly compared with the other two. In any event I consider the clear-toned flowers to be more suitable for distant effect than the bicolors.

Needless to add, there are dozens of other types in my garden, but however good the flower may be, I have little regard for a narcissus which is slow of increase, has a poor constitution, or has flowers that fade in the sun. After all, a bloom is primarily intended to decorate the garden, not a show bench.

How variable colour is! Every spring I see in the shops boxes of that wonderful variety Fortune, each cup a glowing orange. I have bought bulbs of this variety from several different suppliers in an endeavour to achieve this colour, but it must be something to do with the soil, or the power of the sun, or both, because the tone of my blooms is much weaker. As a garden narcissus I find Fortune too tall. Vigour it indisputedly possesses but a rainy, squally day, such as we often experience in March and April, will find a large number of these beautiful flowers face downwards on the surface of the soil, their stems snapped straight off. In my opinion, for small town gardens, such hybrids as February Gold, March Sunshine, Peeping Tom and Tresamble would be far more suitable.

Among my favourite narcissi for the more cultivated parts of the garden are Fleurimont and Fermoy, the first a strikingly clear yellow with frilled orange cup, and the second, white with an orange-red cup. As with most plants with such numbers of varieties, it is perhaps better to choose those you yourself prefer, either at a flower show or by seeing them growing in other gardens.

You will find Bear's Grass, or camassias, listed in most bulb catalogues. The flowers of the commonest form, *Camassia quamash*, are a rather pucy pale blue and the stems are inclined to sprawl. They have increased well here and are quite useful for cut flowers as they appear in June when most of the spring bulbs are over. I am now trying two additional ones, *C. cusickii* and *C. leichtlinii caerulea*, of more erect habit. The first of these has paler flowers than the other, but they both grow to 2–3ft.

Another summer-flowering small bulb which is both charming and practically indestructible, in spite of the rough treatment it receives, is the Star of Bethlehem, *Ornithogalum umbellatum*. This belongs to the same genus as the chincherinchees, and all ornithogalums look much alike, in that they are all white. *O. umbellatum* has foliage like a very glossy crocus leaf. It is a pretty flower for the rougher parts of the garden, is happiest in full sun and increases rapidly. It rarely opens before noon and is back to bed by the early afternoon but, even so, I am happy to have it. *O. pyramidale* has been with me a number of years but does not increase at all. In early June it produces a few white blossoms on 18-inch spikes. Two other species that I planted last year, *O. arabicum* and *O. nutans* came up but did not flower and I am not too optimistic about keeping them.

Camassia quamash

For late summer there is an attractive bulbous plant known as the Cape Hyacinth, *Galtonia candicans*. Many years ago I bought six of these. Coming in August or September, they are useful planted in the shrubbery where their white flowers tinged with green show up well, particularly among purple-leaved plants.

Many people are astonished to see crocuses in the garden in late autumn. The two I grow are *Crocus speciosus* and *C. s. albus*. While they do not seem to increase at the same rate as the spring-flowering forms, they never fail to appear in their season. I have heard it said that the fragility of their stalks makes them look naked and that they soon blow over. For those who think this, there is always the possibility of growing them among rock plants. Some of mine are growing through carpets of *Erica carnea* and look surprisingly effective when they open their lovely flowers to the sun on a mild October day.

Of the larger autumn crocuses, or colchicums, I have in my garden *Colchicum atropurpureum*, *C. speciosum*, Lilac Wonder and other hybrids which, I am afraid, are all mixed up now. The double forms are a more difficult problem for me and I cannot manage to get them to flower. I grow them in good loam in the shade of trees, and I cannot understand why they should be different from the singles, which thrive in such positions. The trouble with all colchicums is the foliage. Appearing in the spring this is rather coarse and looks ugly among the smaller bulbs.

The first time I saw the hardy cyclamen, or sowbread, I was enchanted and have remained so ever since. Unfortunately, the only species that I can keep for any length of time is *Cyclamen neapolitanum*, or the Ivy-leaved Cyclamen. The white form of this, *C. n. album*, is even more appealing than the pink, although both are exquisite.

There is much more chance of getting these cyclamens established if they are grown from seed. The dry corms often never come to life at all and account for many failures and loss of enthusiasm. The seed is expensive but germinates quite easily so that it is well worth while having a go. Failing this, there are specialist firms which provide plants already growing in pots, and for the impatient gardener this is probably the best method of obtaining a reliable stock.

PLANTS REFERRED TO IN THIS CHAPTER

Name	*Origin of species*	*Height*	*Remarks*
Camassia			
cusickii	Oregon	2–3ft.	Pale blue flowers, June/July.
leichtlinii caerulea		2–3ft.	Darker blue flowers, June/July.
quamash	W. North America	2–3ft.	Pale blue flowers, June/July.
Chionodoxa			
gigantea	Asia Minor	6in.	Soft violet-blue flowers, white centre, March/April. Lovely.

Name	*Origin of species*	*Height*	*Remarks*
Chionodoxa			
luciliae	Turkey	6in.	Intense blue flowers with white centre, March/April.
Pink Giant		8in.	Mauve-pink flowers with white centre, March/April.
sardensis	Asia Minor	6in.	Porcelain blue flowers with small white eye, March/April.
Colchicum			
atropurpureum	,,	6in.	Reddish-magenta flowers, autumn.
speciosum			Violet-mauve flowers, autumn.
Lilac Wonder		9–12in.	
Crocus			
chrysanthus			Pale blue with orange stigmata,
Blue Pearl		3–4in.	February.
Cream Beauty		,,	Pale creamy-yellow, orange stigmata, February.
E. A. Bowles		,,	Deep butter yellow, orange stigmata, February. An outstanding variety but the mice love it too!
speciosus	S. Russia, Asia Minor, Persia	4in.	Deep mauve-blue, August to October.
albus		,,	Pure white with orange stigmata.
sieberi			
Violet Queen		3–4in.	Bluish-mauve with orange throat, February.
tomasinianus	Dalmatia	4–8in.	Pale mauvish-blue on the outside of the three outer petals, the inside of the flower and the three inner petals bright lilac-mauve. Delightful. February.
Barr's Purple		4–6in.	Rich purple-lilac inside, February. Very fine.
Taplow Ruby		4–6in.	Dark reddish-purple, smaller flower, February.
Whitewell Purple		4–6in.	Purplish-mauve, February.
Cyclamen			
neapolitanum	S. Europe	4–6in.	Deep pink flowers from July/November. Beautiful marbled leaves.
album		4–6in.	Lovely white flowers. Another treasure.
Eranthis hyemalis	W. Europe	4in.	The Winter Aconite. Yellow flowers, from February/March.
Erythronium			
dens-canis	Europe, Asia to Japan	6–8in.	White and pale mauvish-pink flowers, March/April. Beautiful leaves blotched with purple-brown. A lovely plant.

Name	*Origin of species*	*Height*	*Remarks*
Erythronium			
revolutum White Beauty		6–9in.	A gem of a plant. Creamy-white flowers are poised over mottled shiny green leaves in April/May. Best in damp shade.
tuolumnense	California	9–12in.	Golden-yellow flowers, April. Glistening unmottled green leaves.
Fritillaria			
imperialis	W. Himalaya	3–4ft.	A magnificent plant with flowers of reddish-orange or deep lemon-yellow. April. I hope readers can grow it.
meleagris	Europe	9–12in.	White or chequered flowers in April.
Galtonia candicans	South Africa	2–4ft.	White flowers tinged with green in August/September. It is recommended that it should be planted 6–7 inches deep and left undisturbed.
Galanthus			
nivalis	France, east to the Caucasus	3–6in.	The Common Snowdrop. February/March.
flore pleno			The double form.
Hyacinthus azureus	Asia Minor	4–8in.	Cambridge blue Grape Hyacinth, March/April.
Leucojum			
aestivum Gravetye		18–24in.	The Snowflake. Like a giant Snowdrop, but with several flowers on a stem. Likes moisture.
vernum	Central Europe	12in.	A delightful plant. Flowers usually solitary appearing February/March.
Muscari			
armeniacum	N.E. Asia Minor	8–10in.	The Grape Hyacinth. Sweetly scented blue flowers, May.
comosum monstrosum		12–15in.	The Feather Hyacinth. Mauvish-blue flowers, May/June.
Narcissus			
asturiensis	Spain, Portugal	2–4in.	Tiny yellow daffodils in February/March. Needs good drainage.
bulbocodium	S. France, Spain, Portugal and N. Africa	6–8in.	The Hoop Petticoat Daffodil. Deep yellow flowers, April. Seeds freely.
citrinus		,,	A lovely pale yellow variety.
cyclamineus	Portugal	4–8in.	This is my favourite among the dwarf species. Deep yellow flowers, February/March. Likes moisture.
February Gold		12–15in.	Nearly as large a flower as the ordinary garden types but perhaps a little more refinement.

Name	*Origin of species*	*Height*	*Remarks*
Narcissus			
cyclamineus			
March Sunshine		12–15in.	Very similar to February Gold. Flowers at the same time for me.
Peeping Tom		12–15in.	This and the previous two hybrids look similar to me. They are all self colours, bright yellow.
Fermoy		15–18in.	Perianth white, corolla orange-red at mouth paling to yellow.
Fleurimont		15–18in.	A most beautiful variety. Frilled yellow perianth and bright tangerine corolla.
Fortune		18–24in.	Perianth soft yellow with orange corolla. A very tall and vigorous variety.
Helios		18in.	Perianth yellow, corolla deeper shade. One of the earliest to flower and does well in rough grass.
Sempre Avanti		15–18in.	Creamy-white perianth, bright orange corolla. A strong looking plant.
Sir Watkin		15–18in.	Perianth yellow, corolla yellow. An old variety but very reliable in rough grass.
triandrus albus		6–9in.	Angel's Tears. Flowers, white, up to six on a stem, May. Good drainage required.
Thalia		12–15in.	Creamy-white flowers, several on a stem, May. A good garden plant.
Tresamble		12–15in.	Similar to Thalia but increases rather more quickly.
Ornithogalum			
arabicum	Mediterranean	1–2ft.	White flowers, summer.
nutans	S. Europe	12–18in.	White flowers, April/May.
pyramidale	Mediterranean	12–18in.	White flowers, April/May.
umbellatum	Europe including Britain. N. Africa	6in.	Our native Star of Bethlehem. White flowers, May.
Scilla			
bifolia	Mediterranean	6–8in.	Blue flowers, March/April.
sibirica	E. Russia, Siberia	6in.	Prussian blue flowers, March/April.
tubergeniana	N.W. Persia	3–4in.	Pale blue flowers, early March.

Name	Origin of species	Height	Remarks
Tulipa			
biflora	Caspian and Caucasus	12in.	Slender flowers, whitish stained with green on outside. Several on one stem. March.
greigii hybrids		12–18in.	Varying shades, red, yellow. Beautifully marked leaves.
praestans	Central Asia	10–12in.	Bright scarlet flowers appearing in April. Several on a stem.
tarda	E. Turkestan	5–6in.	Attractive dwarf species with bunch of small yellow and white flowers on each stem. Late April to early May.

CHAPTER NINE

Roses, Climbing and Wall Plants

Roses that down the alleys shine afar,
And open, jasmine-muffled lattices.
And groups, under the dreaming garden-trees,
And the full moon, and the white evening star.
Matthew Arnold

Roses are, indeed, a thorny problem for me because, try as I may, I can admire only some of them. Necessary they may be in the garden but, oh, what a bother to grow them well. As I make this criticism I am reminded of the teacher marking the conduct sheet of one of my friend's children: 'Behaviour, nought out of ten, but we all love him.'

Every rose of the hybrid tea or floribunda type requires attention. Each must be pruned, sprayed, dead-headed and fed, to give of its best. I shall not mention many varietal names of these types as roses are shrubs for selection by the individual, and the best way to choose them is to go to see them growing at a nursery, although the catalogues are most helpful, of course. The number of varieties available is bewilderingly large. They seem to be introduced each year in their dozens, and no sooner is one up-to-date than one is out-of-date again.

For garden decoration, I prefer the floribunda and smaller polyantha types, for the masses of colour they provide when grown in shrubberies and even in herbaceous borders. They also have another great advantage over the hybrid tea roses. Instead of bearing two crops of bloom in one season, they usually manage to flower successionally throughout the summer, and, as I write these words at the end of November, there are nearly as many flowers to be seen as there were in the earlier part of the year. They come at a time when the spring-flowering shrubs are over and are invaluable in positions where later interest is needed. After all, in a small garden, particularly in an industrial area, colour is of primary importance.

These roses should be planted to obtain blocks of colour. Put a handful of peat and bonemeal into the hole when planting, and plant as many bushes of the same variety in each block as you have the space and money for. Three of one variety planted together are infinitely preferable to three different kinds, each with its own individual habit and colour.

As to the pruning, I follow the advice I once read, which said never leave wood more than three years old in the bush. When I prune them in the spring, I usually take off about one-third of each stem to an outward pointing bud, removing any three-year-old wood entirely and also taking out any weak shoots. In this way I have found that I still have some extremely vigorous floribunda rose bushes in the garden that are well over 20 years old.

I have pruned all the bushes in my garden, including the hybrid tea roses, just whenever I have had the time, sometimes in the autumn, sometimes in January or February. Experience has proved to me that the best time to prune them is just as the buds start moving into growth, but before they have had time to make shoots of any length. This really makes sense, as it seems wrong to allow the bushes to expend energy in making growth that has to be cut off, and would be far better employed in the making of sturdy shoots from a limited number of buds. I have found on the occasions when I have pruned my roses in the early part of the winter, that the amount of die-back has been proportionately higher than when I have pruned them in the early spring. However, I do not wish to enter into the controversies which arise when the pruning of roses comes under discussion, as I am well aware that circumstances vary from district to district.

In passing, I cannot remember ever having lost a bush of a floribunda rose, which is another point in their favour. I have found, too, that the hybrid tea roses of Peace parentage are, on the whole, both tough and vigorous.

One good point about growing roses of any kind in an industrial area is that there is no black spot. This is due, I am told, to the presence of sulphur fumes in the atmosphere. There is, however, plenty of mildew, although one would have thought that the same rule would have applied. I recall a large bed of Else Poulsen roses that seemed to be permanently afflicted, in spite of being well sprinkled with flowers of sulphur throughout the season. The plants were growing, too, in the open sunny spot so beloved of the experts. Later I discovered that this is a mildew-prone variety, which is a pity as otherwise it is a very good garden plant.

Taste is such an individual thing that, at the risk of unpopularity,

I must admit to being far from fond of that much acclaimed variety, Fashion. I remember buying, at great expense, six of these bushes when they were first introduced. To my horror I discovered that Fashion clashed unfashionably with every pink flower in the garden and considered myself fortunate in being able to dispose of them to an enthusiast. Later I read that it was advisable to grow this variety in splendid isolation with an evergreen background, but within a small area this could be something of a problem.

Apart from colour clashes—and I am often being told that colours in the garden do not clash—there is also the question of the retention of dead flowers among the newly opened ones. This is a most aggravating fault with roses of the Rumba type, as the petals turn all sorts of hideous colours with age, so that constant attention is required to keep a bed of them looking fresh and attractive. This is no problem with the rose species, but there are few of these that have done really well here.

One of the best is *Rosa moyesii* Geranium, which I grew from seed received from the Royal Horticultural Society's gardens at Wisley a number of years ago. *R. moyesii* itself, grown well, is a most lovely shrub, attaining a height of about 10 feet in some gardens and covered with attractive blood-red flowers, each with a boss of golden stamens. These are followed by large, scarlet, goblet-shaped hips, making a wonderful picture in the autumn. Geranium has made a thicker set bush than its parent, being about 6 feet high and 4 feet through. It has taken many years to produce a really good crop of flowers and would, I am sure, enjoy a milder climate.

Rosa hugonis is most appealing, with dainty fern-like foliage, producing liberally in May masses of small, pale yellow, single blooms. This species never fails to give pleasure, although it is not of vigorous growth here due, perhaps, to the fact that it is in the shrubbery and gets little attention. As in the case of *R. moyesii,* it is a native of China and takes its name from a missionary, Father Hugh Scallon (Pater Hugo), who originally sent seed to England. *R. macrantha* makes a nice bush of 5 feet or more and covers itself in mid-summer with a profusion of showy single flesh-tinted flowers, each with golden stamens. I find this does quite well and consider it to be a lovely shrub.

When I first started gardening I was lured into planting a specimen of *R. omeiensis pteracantha,* on account of the remarkable blood-red, wing-like spines produced the whole of the way up the stems. My plant grew extremely vigorously, but in this carbon-laden atmosphere the

Sedum maximum atropurpureum, a striking plant with its purple foliage and pinkish-bronze flowers

Right: The Lavender Cotton, *Santolina chamaecyparissus*, is a very pretty silver-foliaged plant

A fine border of *Hosta fortunei albopicta* backed by Irish Yews

Hosta glauca is a handsome plantain lily whose leaves have a grape-like bloom on them

thorns were anything but decorative and the prickly bush so altogether unapproachable that it was pulled up and consigned to the bonfire. Such shrubs are not for small intimate gardens. *R. willmottiae* is another delightful rose with foliage similar to, but rather more glaucous than, that of *R. hugonis*. The small, single purplish-rose flowers are charming, but this species found the climate unsuitable and died some years ago. *R. spinosissima altaica*, a hybrid of the Scotch or Burnet rose, has done quite well, running about all over the shrubbery and producing abundantly in May its single creamy-white flowers. This tendency to run about should be noted as I do not think this is a variety suitable for small gardens.

My criticism of the rose species generally is that they have only one period of bloom and, for me, they either run all over the garden and are a nuisance, or they just refuse to do much at all. Had I paid a little more attention to the countries of origin when I was making my purchases, my selections might have been more fortunate, but here again, this is the kind of mistake that every beginner makes. It is, too, quite an understandable one, as the hardiness of the hybrid roses is always being emphasised and the amateur is inclined to extend this qualification to the rose species as a whole.

I remember going to Kew many years ago and seeing a magnificent rose climbing to the top of a tall tree. It bore a heavy crop of the most beautiful white-petalled flowers, each with a golden boss. Coming home full of enthusiasm, I put in an order for *R. moschata*, the Musk rose. When the bush arrived in November, it was planted with due ceremony at the foot of a *Prunus subhirtella autumnalis*, where it has sulked for upwards of 20 years without so much as producing a flower. *R. moschata* hails from the Middle East to North India and China, and although it has been cultivated in England for hundreds of years it is not one of the hardiest species.

But my favourite shrub roses are to be found among the hybrids of this lovely musk rose, such as Cornelia, Felicia and Moonlight. They are all deliciously fragrant, asking for nothing more than a light trimming in the spring and invariably producing masses of flowers, often followed by a second crop in the autumn. Moreover, any non-flowering shoot pulled off with a heel in July and placed in a pot of sandy soil, will root most obligingly.

There are many new hybrid shrub roses being recommended to us nowadays and were I beginning again I should be tempted to try such varieties as Frühlingsmorgen, Nevada and Canary Bird. After seeing a wonderful coloured illustration, I have just planted a specimen of Cocktail in the hope that it will fulfil all the encomiums handed out to it. Certainly it has most attractive, successional bicoloured flowers of red and gold, but, with age, they fade to a rather dingy shade of crimson. It would appear that flowers lack the secret of eternal youth just as humans do.

Of climbing roses, much has been written and said about Mermaid, that very thorny, single, pale yellow rose that is considered by many rosarians to be the peer of them all. Here it took years to settle down on a west wall and the winter of 1962–63 put it right back to where it started from when it was planted. Admittedly it has been neglected, but it has done little to justify the extravagant claims made for it and, in this part of the world, one of the more ordinary climbing roses would probably give a far better display.

Of the rambling roses, my first choice must surely be Albertine, with coppery-pink flowers and the attractively tinted foliage that so admirably blends with them. As it had done so well with me I was astonished to find that the very severe winter just referred to killed several specimens outright and cut others down to ground level.

For delicacy of colour and prolific growth the pale pink Dr W. Van Fleet is a most charming variety and far more satisfactory than the perpetual-flowering New Dawn. The lovely Emily Gray found the soil too cold and left many years ago, but this yellow rose, with its beautiful glossy green leaves, should certainly be included in the list of anyone who can grow these plants really well.

The unusual coral-pink Thelma also disliked the cold and dwindled and died. I do not think this is a vigorous variety and it seems to be more suitable for a pillar than a pergola. Easlea's Golden Rambler, in spite of a slow start, has made a good pillar rose, and although the winter of 1962–1963 cut it to the ground, it appears to have been given a new lease of life and it is now growing vigorously once more. The indestructible Dorothy Perkins and Sanders' White are both here and provide welcome masses of colour when the larger flowered ramblers are over.

Of the climbing tea roses, Allen Chandler is a fine, vigorous scarlet which never fails to please me. It is semi-double but it is, as far as I am concerned, the best of all the reds. I cannot find it in my heart to admire the rather harsh tone of Chaplin's Pink Climber, although it is doing well on a north wall. Climbing Peace planted 10 years ago, pruned, manured and tended, has achieved no more than that number of flowers in as many years. Do not tell me how to make it flower. Other varieties bloom for me and so should this. The tendency to blindness is noticeable in the bush form and seems to have become accentuated in the climber.

Lady Waterlow and Phyllis Bide make better pillar roses, as here they have not reached more than 5 or 6 feet in height. Neither have Lady Sylvia or Le Rêve done much better as climbers. Were I beginning again, I should be inclined to try some of the newer hybrids, such as Danse du Feu, Maigold or Tropique. I always say that I am going to do away with roses altogether, as they are such enemies of stockings and clothes in general, and are such unpleasant subjects to prune, but I never seem to carry out my threats. All this sounds as though I do not like roses as flowers at all, but I love to see huge bowls of their sweetly perfumed blooms scattered about the house.

The next most popular climbing plant must surely be the clematis. The lovely *C. montana* and its variety *rubens* are perfectly hardy. I remember seeing this plant growing in Ireland the whole height of a most enormous Irish Yew, and how marvellously natural it looked! I am trying the same trick by growing a specimen over one of my conifers, but it is outgrowing its host and will, I think, end up by smothering it altogether. Still, I like the idea and think that this plant should be used more often to climb up evergreen trees, especially in industrial areas where the foliage is often so dingy. *C. montana* flowers prolifically in May, and even young plants are covered with blossom.

The larger-flowered hybrid clematis also grow quite well here once they become established. I am trying these too, growing them among trees, as they bloom later than *C. montana*. I have planted one at the foot of a *Prunus* Amanogawa, which needs brightening up after its flowering season is over. Everyone knows that clematis like their feet in the shade and their heads in the sun and I try to give them these conditions. They are also said to prefer lime in the soil, but *C. montana* seems to grow quite well in our neutral loam. I have been surprised, in an agreeable sort of way, to find that clematis are quite happy at the foot of a north-facing wall.

The common honeysuckle, *Lonicera periclymenum*, will also do well in this position and when in flower will help to disguise some of the disagreeable scents pervading the 'modern' countryside, due to the use of slaughterhouse refuse as manure.

A useful wall shrub is the Firethorn, *Pyracantha coccinea lalandii*, which is, of course, equally happy growing in an open position. Here it grows quite well on a west wall, and if the lateral shoots are kept pruned, its flowers and berries give good displays. A yellow-berried variety, Knap Hill Buttercup, has been most disappointing. It is on the same wall and during its 15 years in this position it has hardly had a respectable crop of its very much smaller berries, so that I intend to replace it with a worthier shrub.

For many years *Jasminum officinale* climbed through a *Cotoneaster horizontalis* and into the red-berried Firethorn, but the winter of 1962 finished it off. The ordinary yellow *J. nudiflorum* does not do well in my garden but, as I have seen some good specimens growing locally, this is probably due to its position on a north wall.

Parthenocissus quinquefolia, or the Virginia Creeper, is another unknown quantity. This grew well on a north wall for several years and then, having climbed to a height of about 12 feet, died during a severe winter. There is quite a good specimen on a south wall in the village in which I live and, growing on a grey-walled farmhouse in the open country nearby, a magnificent plant that never fails to stand out in the autumn scene.

Of the most vigorous climber of all, the Russian Vine *Bilderdyckia* (*Polygonum*) *baldschuanicum*, I hardly dare speak. This may be excellent for covering unsightly objects, but it is not suitable for small gardens. It grows rampantly practically everywhere and not only hides the unsightly object, but often ends up by nearly carrying it away as well. Of course, it is excellent when trained up the stump of a dead tree and is always better growing in an open position.

I do not think that I have seen a really good specimen of *Wisteria sinensis* growing locally. This is a most popular climber and doubtless is quite easy to keep within bounds when it has lost its youthful vigour, but it has seemed to me to be a most energetic plant, and if not regularly trained and pinched back will soon become a tangled thicket of shoots, on a rather grander scale than an untrained clematis. I may be misjudging the wisteria, but the owner of the one I have in mind seems to spend half the summer months climbing up and down a ladder, or risking his neck, or those of his friends, by leaning out of the bedroom windows in an endeavour to control the exuberant new growth. Possibly a better plan, if you have the space and the will power to start with a young plant, would be to train it so that it falls over a wall and can be more easily dealt with.

Another climber growing locally, although not in my own garden, is the Climbing Hydrangea, *Hydrangea petiolaris*. This attaches itself to the wall in the manner of ivy and is most effective when flowering in July. A similar plant, but with a more handsome creamy-white inflorescence, is *Schizophragma hydrangeoides*. I have recently planted a specimen of this at the foot of a shady wall in a local garden and, although it is only small, it appears to be doing well. Both of these climbers come from Japan and are deciduous.

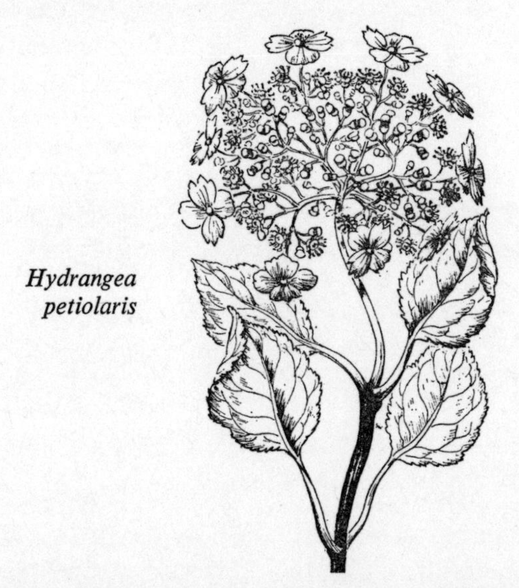

Hydrangea petiolaris

I am making a second attempt to establish a plant of *Actinidia kolomikta*. This climbing shrub, which is a native of China and Japan, eventually reaches a height of about 20 feet. When young it has purplish foliage but later in the season it assumes a tri-coloured variegation, the terminal sections of the leaves often becoming chalk white.

I have not been encouraged to grow climbers on the walls of the house and many others oppose the idea. Where there is no objection, the easiest way to train such plants is to attach coarse pig netting to the walls, to which the growing shoots can readily be tied. This is a longer lasting and much simpler method than that of using wall nails which, by their constant addition and renewal, do far more damage to the cement in the interstices.

There are many shrubs which make good wall plants and are commonly seen growing in this position. I have already mentioned cotoneaster and chaenomeles in another chapter, but so far I have not spoken of *Kerria japonica pleniflora*, the Jew's Mallow. This is a bush that can quite well be grown in the open, but the plant I most admire is the one growing in the village on a south-facing wall where, in April and May, it makes a cheerful picture with its bright orange-yellow flowers set against the emerald green leaves. I grew this shrub on a south wall for a little while, but it was a draughty position and the blooms were few and the tips of the branches always brown. Rather than throw it away altogether I divided my plant into three portions, which I pushed down the garden under a horse chestnut tree. These bushes are now growing in shade and rough grass but manage to do as well there as did the original kerria on the draughty wall. *K. japonica* itself has single yellow flowers and is preferred by some people; it certainly makes a neater, less lanky bush than the double variety. There are also two variegated forms, one with yellow-margined leaves and the other with white-margined ones.

Caryopteris x *clandonensis* is a doubtfully hardy shrub in this part of the North, but it is useful for later summer effect, having cymes of bright blue flowers and dull green leaves. It makes only a small plant of 3 to 5 feet in height and is easily propagated by half-ripe cuttings. If grown against a wall, there is a better chance of survival, although I have never kept it more than a year or two.

The Plumbago, *Ceratostigma willmottianum*, is a similar shrub although hardier than the caryopteris, and has darker blue flowers borne in terminal clusters that open in the later summer and autumn months. Very often it dies down completely during the winter and I think that I have lost it, only to find it sprouting from the base again the following spring. I find this a rather disappointing plant as it is inclined to produce its flowers in ones or twos and has never given what I would call a really good display.

I have tried the Californian Lilac, *Ceanothus* Gloire de Versailles, several times, as I have seen a specimen growing well only 10 miles away, but have been forced to admit defeat.

Hydrangeas are excellent wall shrubs as also are several of the grey-foliaged plants that are doubtfully hardy in the open garden. Some of the more tender bulbs could be tried in such a position. I have been given some nerines, but cannot make up my mind whether I dare risk them outside at all. If I do, it will be at the foot of my sunny west wall where some of the tulip species are growing. For many years I attempted to flower *Iris unguicularis* at the foot of a south wall but without success, so gave it up as a bad job and threw the plant away. Then I read an article which said that the solution to this problem was to obtain a piece of a plant that was known to flower regularly. My sister in Eastbourne, who has a large clump, very kindly obliged, and I planted her offering close to a tender rarity I am attempting to establish, *Piptanthus laburnifolius*. Now this Evergreen Laburnum, as it is called, which I had grown from seed and planted out the previous autumn, had survived the winter and was looking quite healthy until I planted the *Iris unguicularis* alongside it. Then, leaf by leaf, it appeared to be vanishing until I suddenly realised that slugs must be consuming it. I promptly put down some slug bait and the following morning, to my amazement, caught the largest snail that I have ever seen. I realised later that this must have been imported with the iris, as, mercifully, we do not have these brutes in this part of Yorkshire, being well satisfied with the many varieties of local slugs.

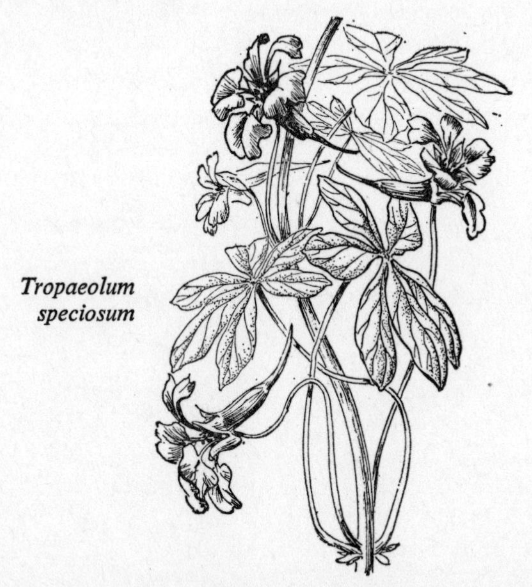

Tropaeolum speciosum

Finally, I must say a word about that temperamental plant, *Tropaeolum speciosum*. The advice given by the experts about this plant, I recall, was to dig a trench 2 feet deep and 1 foot wide, do this and that, and plant the thong-like roots of the Flame Flower gingerly at the bottom of the trench when, in time, you would find that you would have masses of scarlet nasturtium-like flowers creeping through the shrubs and trellises. Trellis was erected, the foundations of the house were excavated, and I waited like an expectant terrier at a rabbit hole. By the close of the following season, a tiny wisp of green, about 2 inches long, had snaked its way out of the soil, on the surface of which it wilted. This performance was repeated the next year, and the next, until the terrier's interest waned. But do not despair. My *Tropaeolum speciosum* emerged right down the garden about 20 yards away and, to this day, I do not know how it did it. I cannot say that it is exactly flourishing either, that would spoil the tale, but it winds itself through a yew hedge, rewarding me with the occasional flash of scarlet in late summer.

PLANTS REFERRED TO IN THIS CHAPTER
[CLIMBING AND WALL PLANTS]

Name	*Origin of species*	*Ultimate height*	*Description*	*Annual rate of growth in author's garden*
Actinidia kolomikta	China, Japan	10–20ft.	Leaves turn red and are chalk white at the apices.	6–9in.
Bilderdyckia baldschuanicum	S. Turkestan	Up to 50ft.	The Russian Vine. Creamy-white flowers, July/October.	
Caryopteris x *clandonensis*		5ft.	Pale blue flowers, August/September.	1–1½ft.
Ceanothus Gloire de Versailles		4–6ft.	Pale blue flowers, June to September.	
Ceratostigma willmottianum	W. China	2–4ft.	Bright blue flowers, July/October.	1–2ft.
Clematis montana	Himalaya	20–30ft.	Covered with white flowers, May.	When established 3–6ft.
rubens		20–30ft.	Covered with pink flowers, May.	3–6ft.
Hydrangea petiolaris	Japan	60–80ft.	White flowers, June. Self-clinging climber.	
Iris unguicularis	Algeria	18in.	Lilac flowers, November/March. Requires a warm sunny spot to flower well.	

Name	*Origin of species*	*Ultimate height*	*Description*	*Annual rate of growth in author's garden*
Jasminum nudiflorum	China	12ft.	The well-known Winter Jasmine. Yellow flowers, November/February.	Poor growth here.
officinale	Persia, N. India, China	Up to 30ft.	White flowers, June/September.	3–5ft.
Kerria japonica	China, Japan	4–6ft.	Single yellow flowers, April/May.	2–3ft.
pleniflora		6–12ft.	Double, orange-yellow flowers, April/May.	1–5ft.
Lonicera periclymenum	Europe, N. Africa, W. Asia	10–20ft.	The Common Honeysuckle. Yellowish-white flowers suffused purple, June/August.	1½–3ft.
Parthenocissus quinquefolia	E. North America	40–50ft.	The Virginian Creeper. Self-clinging with wonderful autumn colour.	
Piptanthus laburnifolius	Himalaya	8–12ft.	The Evergreen Laburnum. Yellow flowers, May.	1–2ft.
Pyracantha coccinea lalandii		Up to 20ft.	The Firethorn. White flowers in June followed by scarlet berries in autumn.	1–2ft.
Schizophragma hydrangeoides	Japan	Up to 40ft.	Yellowish-white bracts July onwards. Self-clinging climber.	
Tropaeolum speciosum	Chile	9–12ft.	Small flame nasturtium-like flowers in August/September. Lovely when you can get it established and never rampant enough to be a nuisance.	
Wisteria sinensis	N. China	Up to 100 ft.	Mauve fragrant flowers in dense racemes 8–12 inches long. May.	

[ROSES]

Rosa	*Type*	
Albertine	Rambler	Double, coppery-salmon.
Allen Chandler	Climber	Semi-double, vivid crimson-scarlet.
Canary Bird	Shrub	Single, deep canary yellow. 5–6ft.
Chaplin's Pink Climber	Rambler	Single, vivid deep pink.
Climbing Lady Sylvia	Climber	Double, deep flesh pink flowers, shaded apricot.
Climbing Peace	Climber	Climbing form of the popular bush rose. Sparse flowering.

Name	*Origin of species*	*Type*	*Description*
Cocktail		Shrub	Crimson and yellow, single flowers. 5–6ft.
Cornelia		Shrub	Musk rose. Double flowers, strawberry pink flushed yellow. Scented. 4–5ft.
Danse du Feu		Climber	Double, orange-scarlet flowers.
Dorothy Perkins		Rambler	Double, pink flowers.
Dr W. Van Fleet		Rambler	Double, flesh pink flowers.
Easlea's Golden Rambler		Rambler	Double, golden-yellow flowers.
Else Poulsen		Floribunda	Single, pink flowers.
Emily Gray		Rambler	Loose-petalled deep yellow flowers.
Fashion		Floribunda	Double, salmon-pink flowers.
Felicia		Shrub	Double, salmon-pink flowers shaded yellow. Sweetly scented. 4–5ft.
Frühlingsmorgen		Shrub	Single rosy-pink flowers with yellow centres. 6ft.
hugonis	Central China	Shrub	Single, yellow flowers in May. Attractive foliage. 8ft.
Lady Waterlow		Climber	Loose-petalled, semi-double flowers of pale salmon-blush. 5–6ft.
Le Rêve		Climber	Large semi-double lemon-yellow flowers.
macrantha		Bush	Single, pale rose maturing to white. Fragrant. 5–10ft.
Maigold		Climber	Double, golden-yellow.
Mermaid		Climber	Single, pale yellow with conspicuous yellow stamens. 20–30ft.
Moonlight		Shrub	Lemon-white, semi-double Musk rose. 4–5ft.
moschata	S. Europe to N. India and China	Climber	The Musk Rose. Pale yellow, single flowers changing to almost pure white in corymbose clusters. 30ft.
moyesii	W. China	Shrub	Single, dark red flowers in June, followed by enormous orange-scarlet hips. 6–10ft.
Geranium		Shrub	Similar to *moyesii* but of bushier growth. 6ft.
Nevada		Shrub	Creamy-white, single flowers. 6–7ft.
New Dawn		Rambler	Shell pink, double flowers fading to blush.
omeiensis pteracantha	W. China	Shrub	Small, single, white flowers. Remarkable for its conspicuous red thorns. 12ft.
Phyllis Bide		Rambler	Small, pale gold, double flowers, flushed carmine and pink. 5–6ft.

Name	*Origin of species*	*Type*	*Description*
Rumba		Floribunda	Yellow flowers flecked and edged with bright red.
Sanders' White		Rambler	Small, white, double flowers.
spinosissima altaica		Shrub	Single, creamy-white flowers in May. Runs all over the garden. 6ft.
Thelma		Rambler	Coral-pink, double flowers.
Tropique		Climber	Double flowers of brilliant scarlet.
willmottiae	W. China	Shrub	Single, purplish-rose flowers in June. Attractive foliage. 5–10ft.

CHAPTER TEN

Herbaceous Perennial Plants

Smile the carnation and the pink;
And down the borders, well I know,
The poppy and the pansy blow . . .
Rupert Brooke

Most people grow what they like to grow in their herbaceous borders and I do not think you will want to hear from me full descriptions of what I think you should put in them. What I am going to do is to tell you about some of the varieties of plants I admire, with a few of the less common ones thrown in.

Nowadays the vogue for the completely herbaceous border is on its way out. I always think in the winter time that it would be better to put something else in the place of ours. However, when it is at its best in the months of June, July and August I reverse my decision.

Herbaceous borders follow the spring bulbs and shrubs, and their display, which begins before the first of the hybrid roses flower, provides the colour masses desired. They do not entail too much work if treated the 'lazy' way. Ours is not even forked over annually and the plants are rarely divided. A mulch of peat thrown on the surface saves a lot of work, provided, of course, that there are no perennial weeds about. Does it matter so much if each flower in a border of this kind is grown to perfection? I do not think so. Perfection is for the specialist. The principal function of my border is colour and if I wish to coddle a particular favourite, then I do not grow it in the competitive border but on its own in another part of the garden. The really hard work is, I find, cutting down and clearing away the dead foliage in the autumn. Staking is rarely a problem either, as the plants grow so closely together that they hold themselves up. A tricky wind will occasionally make a channel here and there but, curiously enough, almost always in the same place so that, over the years, one becomes more or less forewarned and can make the necessary provision.

One of my favourite border plants is *Geranium psilostemon.* It has a colour described as magenta-red, and I dare say this is correct but, to me, it is that peculiar and uncommon light purplish-red colour of some of the St Brigid anemones. The black-centred flowers rise in masses over the decoratively divided leaves, so that it is a most lovely plant, either in or out of bloom. It has the pleasing habit, if not dead-headed, of seeding itself freely so that you may form a colony somewhere else in the garden, although this is another of those perennials for which there is always a queue waiting. As it will grow in the semi-shade, I am putting all the seedlings I can rescue into the woodland garden, together with a few plants of *G. pratense album plenum* and *G. p. coeruleum plenum*. I have one criticism of these geraniums and that is that they appear to be very prone to attack by caterpillars of the gooseberry sawfly type which, if allowed to feed unchecked, can destroy the foliage effect in no time at all.

Black-eyed Susan, *Rudbeckia speciosa* (*R. newmanii*), should be a first choice in any selection of garden perennials. This is a magnificent plant, throwing up in the autumn its bright, black-centred golden flowers on stiff stems. It looks lovely growing in association with the deep wine-coloured *Aster* Winston Churchill. Admittedly it is shallow rooting and easily smothered in a highly competitive border but, as I mentioned previously, plants such as these are better on their own. The rudbeckias, or cone-flowers as they are also called, dislike drought, but once they find conditions to their liking, they soon form fine clumps. I am told that *R. sullivantii* Goldsturm is a superior form, but I find *R. speciosa* difficult to improve upon.

Salvia x *superba* is another must. This plant does not seem very fond of heavy clay loam and is apt to die off in severe winters. It also dislikes being divided. To propagate it I pull off some of the lateral stem shoots when they are about 3 inches long, putting them into my usual pot of sandy soil. They root in no time and I have a nice batch of young plants, under glass, ready for any contingency. As ideal conditions, this member of the sage family likes light soil and a place in the sun. Once you have it in your garden you will fall a victim to its charm and will never want to be without it. It comes into bloom in July, the lovely violet-blue labiate flowers being borne in spikes. The leaves and, indeed, the whole plant, are delightfully fragrant. It is quite happy in the herbaceous border but is also worth growing in a more isolated position.

The Golden Rod or solidago is a plant often held in low esteem by gardeners, sometimes I think because it is almost too easy to grow.

Many varieties that people give you when you first start a garden are extremely poor, but there is one which I think is superb and so good that I grow it on its own so that people can take a good look at it. This is *Solidago* Goldenmosa, which is one of the dwarfer growing kinds. It does not creep at the same rate as some of the other varieties and, as the name suggests, it has flowers which look rather like mimosa. In addition to this, however, and this is the attraction for me, when the flowers are in the bud stage the leaves take on the same colour, so that the whole plant is a mass of pale gold. The very tall variety Golden Wings is one of the finest hybrids for the back of the border. It blooms late in the year, usually in mid-October, and is most useful for mixing with the later asters.

The oriental poppies, varieties of *Papaver orientale*, are among the most flamboyant of flowers, but are easily blown over by the wind and become extremely untidy when their display is finished. There is a variety, however, named Mrs Perry, of the most delicate shade of pink, with more wind-resistant stems.

Another thing I have noticed about these poppies is that they stand the wind better when the clumps are smaller, in which case it would probably be better to divide them regularly, substituting say, three small plants for one large one. All the oriental poppies make glorious cut flowers, remaining fresh for several days if picked in the bud. Originally I bought a packet of seeds and now have quite a selection of colours. Some of them have smoky white petals with purple centres, while others have fringed petals of the most subtle hues. If you do grow them from seed, be sure to keep only the best coloured seedlings. I found that among mine there was a deep crimson variety that faded to a most horrible shade of brown after being exposed to only a few hours of sunlight, and wondered who had been responsible for the selection of the seed. Place all these plants in positions where you will be certain that their straggly dying foliage will be well hidden by later flowering perennials.

Numbers of gardeners do not seem to like the Stonecrop or sedum family. Admittedly some of them are little more than weeds in a well-organised garden, but here I will deal with the varieties I like and grow.

Pride of place must be given to *Sedum spectabile*. What other plant in the garden will survive neglect and give such a bountiful display of bloom in the most impossible of situations? It starts its year in March, when the light green, fleshy leaves peer sturdily through the soil. Slowly and neatly it emerges, until, in late September, its large, flat pink heads reach their full beauty. Best grown in the sun and in a lighter soil than I can offer it, this sedum still manages to put most of the other plants in flower at this time of the year in the shade from the point of view of display. Here is a plant which is virtually indestructible. I have dug it up and left the roots out of the soil all the winter, only to find it sprouting again the following spring. It has several hybrids, among them Brilliant, Carmen and Meteor, all in varying shades of pink. Divide it occasionally when the crown looks woody and bless whoever introduced it to gardens.

A hybrid of *S. spectabile*, Autumn Joy, attracts a good deal of attention. This variety with salmon-rose flowers is a distinct colour break. With me, this plant grows to about the same height as the type, but in other gardens I have seen it growing taller.

Sedum telephium was introduced into the garden a few years ago and has surprised me by the liberality with which it seeds itself. It is not such a showy plant as *S. spectabile*, but in certain autumn lights the flower heads of this species are startling in the intensity of their colour, normally a dull red. There is a striking variegated form of this, *S. t.*

Tradescantia virginiana

variegatum, which I have mentioned in my chapter on foliage effects (p. 165). All of these stonecrops seem to have an irresistible appeal to butterflies on sunny days, their heads being crowded with Red Admirals and Peacocks.

The spiderwort, *Tradescantia virginiana*, is a more unusual border plant. In spite of the fact that they may be growing its relative, the Wandering Jew, in pots in the house, you will find that lots of people do not know it. The flowers of the spiderworts vary in colour from snow-white, white with a feathery central tuft of blue, through pale blue to dark blue and magenta. They are not tall plants, are very hardy and have the most uncommon three-petalled blooms which, although they do not last individually for more than a day, put up a display which goes on for weeks. I do not find it necessary to stake my tradescantias, but I have heard that some people do. As with the oriental poppies, I feel that the flower stems may be sturdier and more wind resistant if the plants are divided regularly.

There are one or two pretty perennial evening primroses that do not seem to be well enough known. *Oenothera fruticosa* is one of these, long lived, perfectly hardy and growing to a height of about 18 inches. Yellow River is said to be an improved form of this species and *O. cinaeus* has outstandingly bright foliage in the spring. All of these open their bright yellow flowers during the day and not, as their common name would suggest, only in the evenings.

Monarda didyma Cambridge Scarlet is the popular Scarlet Bergamot, admired by all. I find this plant most difficult to keep for any length of time, as it is shallow rooting and, unless it is mulched, it soon fades away. It is, however, well worth the trouble of topdressing as it has aromatic foliage and is one of the few herbaceous perennials of its colour. It likes a fair amount of moisture and grows well in the shade.

The campion, *Lychnis chalcedonica*, is another valuable scarlet-flowered plant, most effective in the border in June and growing to about 2 feet in height. Not so well known is *L. viscaria splendens flore-pleno*, which is a smaller campion of about 12 inches and one of which I am very fond. As it is not long lived, it is best to detach a few of the crowns from the old plant each year. These root readily in sandy soil and a good stock may be rapidly built up by this method. The double pink Ragged Robin flowers are always admired. Here again, I think this is better grown away from a herbaceous border.

The Woundwort, *Stachys macrantha superba*, has coarse-looking leaves but surprises one by producing stout heads of nettle-like flowers in a most appealing shade of mauve. Do not overlook this sturdy and hardy front row plant. It flowers in June and reaches a height of about 18 inches.

Polygonum bistorta superbum is one of the bistorts or knotweeds which also flowers in June. I first saw this plant in Ireland several years ago and think that at last I have succeeded in obtaining it, although I am still not sure. The variety I saw had stiff stems and terminal spikes of pale pink. There is a darker flowered knotweed which flowers later and is a fine border perennial. This is *P. amplexicaule atrosanguineum.*

There is hardly a garden without the Catmint or *Nepeta mussinii* and how lovely this looks as an edging plant. Most of us also grow *N.* Six Hills Giant which is very much taller. However, not many people know the Calamint, *Calamintha alpina.* This is a similar dwarf plant that flowers from June to the end of August and would be most useful, perhaps, for a small garden.

If you like Forget-me-nots later in the year, you may like to grow the Hound's Tongue, *Cynoglossum nervosum.* This is not long lived, but seeds itself freely, persisting for many years before finally dying out. It is well worth growing for the intensity of colouring of its blue flowers. Grown in association with the polyantha pompon rose Coral Cluster, it is quite delightful and I imagine it would look lovely with white roses too.

The campanulas, or Bell-flowers, are found in one form or another in every garden. For the middle of the border those of the *persicifolia* type are probably the best. *C. glomerata superba,* with clusters of bright violet bells, is a good one for the front row and was the first campanula I acquired. There are now two improved forms of this, Joan Elliott and Purple Pixie.

The less common *C. lactiflora* hybrids are my personal choice in herbaceous bell-flowers. They are very showy for the back of the border. *C. lactiflora* Pritchard's Variety is a deeper blue than the type, while Loddon Anna is a pale pink form. There is also a neat one of only 9 inches, called Pouffe, with light blue flowers, but I have not tried this yet. All these campanulas do well in shade and are suitable for planting in shrubberies for summer effect.

The Orange Sunflower, *Heliopsis* Golden Plume, is a striking autumn-flowering perennial which has recently caught my eye. I have obtained a few plants and am waiting to see whether it will be hardy here as I have had plants of this family in the garden before and lost them. It reaches a height of about 4 feet.

The kniphofias, or Red Hot Pokers as they are usually called, are invaluable subjects for planting in borders or on the edge of woodland. Some of the smaller varieties, such as *K. nelsonii*, have not proved hardy, probably because I have not given them a situation that is well enough drained.

There are many plants that I consider unsuitable for inclusion in herbaceous borders. Some of them are shade lovers, or have an unsophisticated charm, or are of architectural quality, demanding positions of isolation. Others are too small for the front of the border, yet do not seem to fit into the rock garden, while some are suitable only for rougher and less hospitable positions. Among these is *Brunnera macrophylla* (*Anchusa myosotidiflora*). This is one of the first herbaceous plants to appear in the spring, throwing up shortish heads of forget-me-not flowers of the same Cambridge blue. It has strong fibrous roots which it digs into the soil, in sun or shade, wet or dry, and is indispensable where a really tough perennial is required for ground cover.

Brunnera macrophylla

A rather smaller plant, of brighter blue, that likes a shady position, with moisture if possible, is the Lungwort, *Pulmonaria angustifolia*.

This looks delightful in association with the varieties of *Erica carnea* edging the shrubbery, and gives a much earlier and showier display than the Spotted Lungwort, *P. saccharata*, with flowers of pale blue and pink. *P. angustifolia* takes a year or two to settle down but the azure blue flowers are one of the pleasures of spring.

The yellow-flowered *Corydalis lutea*, 9 to 12 inches tall, has attractive rather fern-like foliage, and although some people consider it a nuisance, on account of the freedom with which it seeds itself, I think it is a most welcome addition to the moister and shadier parts of the garden.

A plant that we all know, with similar foliage, is the common Bleeding Heart, *Dicentra eximia.* I used to think that this species should be banished, but have grown to love it and plant it widely under trees and shrubs. Its graceful puce-pink flowers persist all through the summer months and, no matter how hard you look, there hardly seems to be a dead one to detract from the freshness of the new blooms. It dies down at the first hint of frost in the autumn, leaving a handful of 'straw' to mark the spot and afford protection for the crowns. There is a white variety of this, *D. e. alba*, that I have recently planted. There is a showy American introduction, too, *D. formosa* Bountiful, with reddish-purple flowers, which I have resolved to obtain.

Dicentra spectabilis, or Dutchman's Breeches, the most beautiful member of the genus, is not hardy with me, so I pot it up and keep it in the cold greenhouse, using it as a room plant when it comes into flower. Roots of *D. spectabilis* can be purchased in the spring. Succulent shoots about 2 inches long taken off when the plant is breaking into growth root readily in a pot of sandy soil.

For daintiness of foliage and all-round charm, I am a devotee of the Barrenwort, Bishop's Hat, or epimedium. I do not know of any perennial plant that gives me more pleasure from the time it appears in the spring until the time it slips away in the autumn. I am sure that I am not alone in this, as I find myself constantly reminded that I have promised a piece to someone or other, and I live for the day when my own stock is on the increase. Two epimediums are in my garden, one with pink flowers, *E.* Rose Queen, my favourite, and the other, with yellow flowers, *E. perralderianum.* The flowers are, to me, unremarkable. It is the leaves about which I rave. Poised on slender stems, they are daintily heart-shaped, with beautiful veining, and are constantly changing their pattern of colour. I seem quite unable to describe them but if you buy a plant or two of this lovely member of the berberis family you will see what I mean. They prefer shade and do best when undivided. This last is a hint to future applicants!

A plant that I have recently seen and admired and must try to obtain is *Vancouveria hexandra*. The foliage is almost as attractive as that of the epimediums but, of course, I do not know whether this perennial will be hardy in my Yorkshire garden. It is said to be shade loving.

The Solomon's Seal, *Polygonatum multiflorum*, is an old-fashioned plant, still unsurpassed in grace, which is just being rediscovered by the

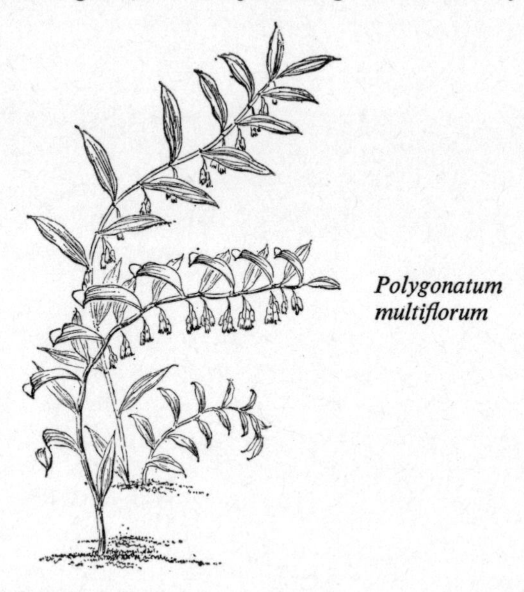

Polygonatum multiflorum

flower arrangers. It likes nothing better than to be left alone in moist shade. Last autumn I fell in love with a variegated form of this, but so far have not been able to secure a root.

The bergenias, formerly known as megaseas, are those plants with huge evergreen leaves and pink flowers, called Elephant's Ears. We see them in most town gardens in the spring looking grimy and forlorn. In other conditions they are magnificent and, indeed, even in industrial areas their flowers are welcome as early in the year as February and March. There are two common kinds, *B. cordifolia* and *B. ligulata*, the first species being slightly earlier than the second. They make good low-foliaged dot plants, or they may be grown *en masse* at the fringe of the woodland. Recently I have been given a crown of *B.* Delbees, a darker flowered form. I am told that this is not so hardy as the others so I shall have to wait and see. As a precaution I have given it winter protection in the form of fern fronds.

For ground cover in the rougher parts of the garden, the Periwinkle, *Vinca minor*, is a good old-fashioned plant. Forming a thick carpet it penetrates even the shadiest of places, smothering the weeds as it goes. I had no idea that there was a double variety until I saw it growing in an Irish garden. There was a huge mass of it, studded with deep purple flowers. To my involuntary, 'Isn't that lovely?' the gardener stooped to pick me a solitary bloom. 'What?' I said, as he handed me the tiny flower, 'No root?' Just as he stooped once more to pick me an infinitesimal scrap, with embryo root attached, I saw, to my horrified gaze, that the garden owner, his wife and the rest of the party were watching the whole pantomime with mild astonishment. After that incident, it was assumed that I should need a pack mule to transport my ill-gotten gains when I landed in England! Nevertheless, this *V. m. multiplex* has done well for me even if it has lost some of the intensity of colour it had when it was growing in the Emerald Isle. Witness of my embarrassment, a friend of mine in the party gave me another piece of this plant as consolation, together with a root of the very pretty *V. m. argenteo-variegata*, the silvery-variegated one with blue flowers.

Other excellent plants for ground cover, such as *Lamium galeobdolon variegatum*, *Lysimachia nummularia aurea*, *Ajuga reptans* and its varieties *multicolor*, *atropurpurea* and *variegata*, *Saxifraga umbrosa*, *Phlox subulata* and so on are referred to in the next chapter on foliage effects.

For a moist shady spot in the garden where a massive plant is required, there is always the Goat's Beard, *Aruncus sylvester*. My specimen is growing alongside the garage, where it can catch all the drips from the roof. It thrives upon neglect and makes a rootstock that would take the muscles of a giant to divide. If happy, by way of a make-weight, it casts its seeds hither and thither so that you, too, can cast bounty upon your friends, without having to disturb the parent plant. I was delighted to see in a garden a smaller version of this, *A. s. kneiffii*, with even more decorative foliage.

Most of the members of the spiraea family like moister conditions than I am able to provide. I do grow a few of the astilbes. At one time these were popular as pot plants, but they appear to have gone out of fashion as such and are more commonly seen in the open garden. The double Meadowsweet, *Filipendula ulmaria flore-pleno*, has a heavy head which lolls over at the first touch of rain. Stake it? Yes, may be for those who boast paid gardeners or have the leisure to do so, but not for the do-it-yourself gardener who is prepared to give the minimum of attention to such tedious chores and prefers to bend his head over the propagating pans.

The genus *Euphorbia*, or Spurge, exercises a strange fascination over me. Most of these are reliably hardy perennials, all the better for being undisturbed. The earliest of those in the garden is *Euphorbia epithymoides*, which 'flowers' in the spring and is about 1 foot high. You will have noticed that I have put the word flowers in quotation marks, as the flowers themselves are insignificant. What you are admiring are the bracts, that is, the part of the plant which surrounds the flowers. In the case of *E. epithymoides* the bracts are bright yellow and curiously enough, in the spring the leaves on the top portion of the plant are infused with the same colour. The florist's Poinsettia, *E. pulcherrima*, is a greenhouse euphorbia, the decorative scarlet bracts being the attractive feature.

Euphorbia griffithii has heads crowned with orange-scarlet and its form Fireglow is said to be an improvement upon it. Growing here in good friable loam, much to my delight it is spreading at a terrific rate by means of underground stolons. I have recently planted *E. sikkimensis*, a most rampant grower I am told, and I intend to collect as many members of this interesting family as I possibly can. The most magnificent of the genus is said to be *E. wulfenii*. I tried this several years ago without much success as it just dwindled away.

If you like the euphorbias, then you will probably be fascinated by such plants as the May Apple, or *Podophyllum emodii*. This enjoys a moist position in peaty soil, which is not surprising when I tell you that it has another name, Ducksfoot. The handsomely cut leaves are dark green mottled with purple and the flowers of either white or pink are followed by large edible fruits. I have not eaten any of these yet as I do not fancy them, but the excuse I give is that I want them for seed. Actually I grew my May Apples originally from seed and they are not large plants. So far the foliage consists of two leaves per specimen, so you can imagine my amazement when I moved one of them last autumn to find that it had a root ball about one foot across. We gardeners are always being told that such and such a plant in the ornamental garden is edible and with the rising cost of living it might not be such a bad idea to lay in a stock of such herbs.

For the wilder and moister parts of the garden again, a good family of plants are the ligularias. The kinds I grow are *Ligularia clivorum*, with plain green leaves, and *L. c.* Othello with green, purple-backed foliage. These are members of the groundsel family and used to be called senecios, and I am always delighted to see their huge heads of orange-yellow flowers open in late August and early September. They are all perfectly hardy and seed themselves freely.

A less well-known Mongolian species is *L. przewalskii.* This has large, well-divided leaves, in the style of ranunculus, quite unlike the

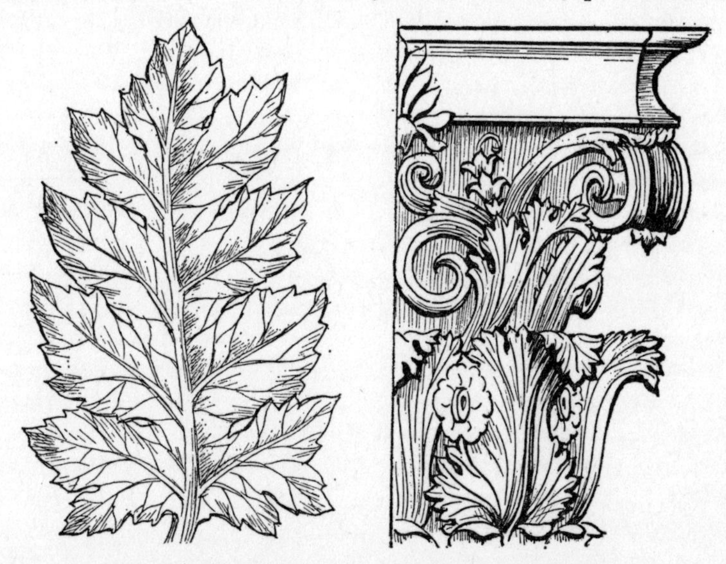

Acanthus leaf, and top of Greek Corinthian column

round leaves of the preceding types, and tapering heads of small deep yellow flowers borne, in June or July, on blackish stems. It is a most showy plant.

The design of the acanthus leaf has been adopted by artists in all mediums all over the world from the most ancient times. This is a most stately plant and throws up heads of whitish-mauve flowers in August. The variety I grow is *Acanthus mollis latifolius*, of striking architectural form. My plants have proved to be slow growing and rather shy in the production of their labiate flowers.

Another genus for which I have the greatest admiration is *Helleborus*. Probably the best-known member is *H. niger*, the Christmas Rose, that low growing, evergreen plant that delights in the shadier parts of the garden, rewarding the owner every year, if it is content, with numbers of snow-white flowers, each with a golden 'boss' of stamens. These are always out in time for Christmas, but the plants go on flowering for several weeks afterwards. The variety named Potter's Wheel has even whiter blooms than the type; it flowers several weeks later. Cloching the plants when the first buds are seen will provide longer flower stems.

Hellebores resent disturbance, so try not to dig them up again once you have decided upon the right spot for their future home. Mine grow in rather heavy soil in the shade of some birch trees and among azaleas, benefiting from the peaty mulches given to the latter.

Helleborus niger is, I think, the most satisfactory of the hellebores here, but I also grow *H. foetidus*, *H. corsicus*, *H. atrorubens* and several plants of the Lenten Rose, *H. orientalis*. *H. atrorubens* thrusts its dark purplish-red flowers out of the soil at about the same time as *H. niger*. The stems are a little longer but it is a sombre bloom at best, and as it hangs its head you do not see its full beauty unless you pick it. *H. corsicus* and *H. foetidus* bear greenish flowers that are the secret of their appeal. After all, how many green flowers are there? Also, in fairness, I must add that the foliage of both plants is extremely decorative.

Helleborus orientalis, flowering later, comes in all shades from greenish-cream to deep purple, some of them having spots. So far my collection comprises a rather drab greenish variety and a dull red one, with various seedlings which have not yet flowered. Whenever I read about these plants I am told that the blooms wilt when picked. I am dissuaded. Mine remain firmly unplucked.

I started this chapter by telling you the lazy way of dealing with a herbaceous border. You may be interested in an idea I had in connection with the disposal of lupin heads. Most of us grow those magnificent Russell hybrids and, lovely as they are when in flower, they look pretty dreadful when the seed pods have formed. I used to collect these dead heads in baskets and dump them, but now I throw them back into the border among the other plants and, believe me, there is no trace of them when the rest of the border is cut down in the autumn. I feel encouraged by this to do the same with all the other dead heads taken off during the summer, but have not done so yet.

PLANTS REFERRED TO IN THIS CHAPTER

Name	*Origin of species*	*Approx. height*	*Remarks*
Acanthus mollis latifolius		3–4ft.	Beautifully cut leaves. White or rose flowers, August.
Ajuga reptans			
atropurpurea		6in.	Bronzy-purple foliage. Blue flowers, May/July.
multicolor		6in.	Bronze leaves with creamy-rose variegation. Blue flowers, June.
variegata		6in.	Green leaves with cream tinged rose variegation. Bright blue flowers, June.
Aruncus			
sylvester	N. America, Europe, Asia	4ft.	Fine foliage plant. Creamy-white flowers, June.
kneiffii		1½–2ft.	A smaller edition of the type.
Aster Winston Churchill		2½ft.	Beetroot purple flowers, September.
Bergenia			
cordifolia	Siberia	1ft.	Reddish flowers, March/April.
Delbees		1½ft.	Dark red flowers, March/April.
ligulata	Nepal	1ft.	Pale pink flowers, March/May.
Brunnera macrophylla	W. Caucasus	1½ft.	Blue flowers, May/June.
Calamintha alpina	S. Europe	6in.	Purplish flowers, July/August. Like a dwarf catmint.
Campanula			
glomerata superba		2½ft.	Bright violet flowers. June/July.
Joan Elliott		1½ft.	Violet-blue flowers, May/June.
Purple Pixie		15in.	Violet-purple flowers, late summer.
lactiflora	Caucasus	3ft.	Pale blue flowers, June/August.
Loddon Anna		3–4ft.	Pale pink flowers, June/August.
Pouffe		9in.	Pale blue flowers, June/August.
Pritchard's Variety		3ft.	Deep blue flowers, June/August.
persicifolia	Europe	1–3ft.	Blue and white flowers, July/August.
Corydalis lutea	,,	9–12in.	Yellow flowers, May/September. Good in shade.
Cynoglossum			
nervosum	Himalaya	1–1½ft.	Blue forget-me-not flowers, July/September.
Dicentra			
eximia	United States	9–18in.	Reddish-purple flowers, all through the summer.
alba		9–18in.	White flowers, all through the summer.
formosa Bountiful		9–18in.	Paler reddish-pink flowers than *eximia*, May/June.
spectabilis	Siberia, Japan	1½–2ft.	Rosy-crimson flowers, May/July.

Name	Origin of species	Approx. height	Remarks
Epimedium			
perralderianum	Algeria	1ft.	Yellow flowers, spring.
Rose Queen		1ft.	Deep pink flowers May/June. Superb foliage.
Euphorbia			
epithymoides	Europe	1–1½ft.	Striking yellow bracts, spring.
griffithii	Himalaya	2ft.	Orange-scarlet bracts, June. Seeds and spreads.
sikkimensis	Sikkim	3ft.	Purplish spring foliage, yellow bracts.
wulfenii	Europe	4ft.	Yellow bracts, June.
Filipendula ulmaria flore-pleno		1½ft.	Double form of Meadowsweet. Cream flowers, July.
Geranium			
pratense album			
plenum		2ft.	Double white flowers, July/August.
coeruleum plenum		2ft.	Double blue flowers, July/August,
psilostemon	Armenia	2–3ft.	Magenta flowers, June/July. All these hardy geraniums have lovely foliage.
Heliopsis Golden Plume		4ft.	Bright double orange-yellow flowers, July/August.
Helleborus			
atrorubens		1ft.	Purplish-red flowers, December/February.
corsicus	Corsica	1½ft.	Yellowish-green flowers, March/April. Lovely foliage.
foetidus	W. and S. Europe	2ft.	Greenish flowers, March/May. Seeds itself freely. Finely cut foliage.
niger	Central and S. Europe and W. Asia	6–8in.	White flowers, December/January. The Christmas Rose.
Potter's Wheel		6–9in.	Even whiter flowers, later than *niger*.
orientalis	Greece, Asia Minor	1–1½ft.	Flowers variable, from greenish-cream to shades of red and purple, sometimes spotted.
Kniphofia nelsonii	Orange Free State	1½–2ft.	Bright scarlet flowers, October.
Lamium galeobdolon variegatum		1–1½ft.	Yellow flowers, summer. Variegated foliage. Good ground cover.
Ligularia			
clivorum	China	3–4ft.	Large orange-yellow flowers, August. Likes moisture.
Othello		3–4ft.	The leaves are purple backed.
przewalskii	Mongolia	4ft.	Yellow flowers with black stems, June/July.
Lychnis			
chalcedonica	E. Russia	2ft.	Scarlet flowers, June/July.
viscaria splendens flore-pleno		1–1½ft.	Double magenta-pink flowers, June.

Name	*Origin of species*	*Approx. height*	*Remarks*
Lysimachia nummularia aurea		Prostrate	The golden form of Creeping Jenny. Yellow flowers, July/August.
Monarda didyma Cambridge Scarlet		2–3ft.	Scarlet flowers, June/September. Likes moisture.
Nepeta			
mussinii	Caucasus, Persia	1–2ft.	Catmint. Mauve flowers, June.
Six Hills Giant		2–3ft.	Mauve flowers, June.
Oenothera			
cinaeus	Extra tropical America	15in.	Golden flowers, June/August. Coloured foliage in spring. Not reliably hardy here.
fruticosa Yellow River		1–1½ft.	Deep yellow flowers, June/September.
Papaver			
orientale	Armenia	2–3ft.	All shades from white to deep crimson in its varieties.
Mrs Perry		2–3ft.	Delightful single pink flowers.
Podophyllum emodii	India	1ft.	Pink or white flowers, May. Attractive foliage.
Polygonatum			
multiflorum	Europe, N. Asia	2–2½ft.	Solomon's Seal. Cream flowers, May and June.
variegatum		2–2½ft.	A wonderfully effective plant. Variegated foliage.
Polygonum			
amplexicaule atrosanguinem		2–3ft.	Red spikes of flowers, August/October.
bistorta superbum		2–3ft.	Pale pink spikes, May/June.
Pulmonaria			
angustifolia	Central Europe	9–12in.	Bright blue flowers, April. Likes moisture.
saccharata	Europe	6–12in.	Pink and blue flowers, April.
Rudbeckia			
speciosa	N. America	1½–2ft.	Golden flowers, August/October. Likes moisture.
sullivantii Goldsturm		1½–2ft.	Orange-yellow flowers, August/September. Likes moisture.
Salvia x *superba*		2–3ft.	Violet-blue flowers, July/September.
Sedum			
spectabile	China	1–1½ft.	Pink flowers, September/October. Likes the sun.
Autumn Joy		1–1½ft.	Bright salmon-rose flowers; a striking plant.
Brilliant		1–1½ft.	Deep rose flowers.
Carmen		1–1½ft.	Bright carmine-rose flowers.
Meteor		1–1½ft.	Carmine-red flowers.

Name	*Origin of species*	*Approx. height*	*Remarks*
Sedum			
telephium		1–1½ft.	Reddish-purple, August/September.
variegatum			Leaves splashed with yellow variegation.
Solidago			
Goldenmosa		2–3ft.	Bright yellow flowers, August/September.
Golden Wings		6ft.	Bright yellow flowers, September/October.
Stachys macrantha superba		1½ft.	Stout heads of lovely mauve flowers, May/June.
Tradescantia virginiana	E. United States	1–1½ft.	White, blue, reddish-purple flowers, June/September.
Vancouveria hexandra	Washington to California	8–12in.	White flowers, May. Dainty foliage.
Vinca			
minor		Trailing	Blue flowers, April/September.
argenteo-variegata			Silver variegation, blue flowers.
multiplex			Double purple flowers.

CHAPTER ELEVEN

Foliage Effects

Then, each in its peculiar honours clad,
Shall publish even to the distant eye
Its family and tribe.

W. Cowper

Silver foliage is a most useful foil in any garden, but it is a fact that in cold gardens plants with silver leaves are inclined to be less hardy than many of the plants with ordinary green ones. In industrial areas where there is a heavy carbon deposit, I think I should say at once that growing plants with silver and coloured foliage will never give the same pleasure that it gives in cleaner districts. Among the evergreens, especially those with silver foliage, being of a more delicate hue than the gold, you will find a disappointing drabness, rather than a sparkling freshness of tone. By contrast, the deciduous plants get a fresh start, as it were, every year and are, on the whole, more satisfactory.

Among the silver-grey- and blue-foliaged trees, I have made reference elsewhere to *Cedrus atlantica glauca*, *Chamaecyparis lawsoniana glauca* Spek, *C. l.* Silver Queen, *C.* Triomphe de Boskoop, *C. l. allumii*, *C. l. fletcheri*, *C. pisifera squarrosa*, *Picea pungens kosteriana*, *Juniperus horizontalis*, *J. communis compressa*, *J. virginiana glauca* and so on, but have not mentioned the Silver-leaved Pear, *Pyrus salicifolia pendula*, a most praiseworthy weeping tree, ideal for the small garden. This has silver willow-like leaves and creamy flowers, and although I do not grow it there is a fair specimen in a local garden.

Everyone knows the lavender, or lavandula, and there are several forms of this with varying colours of flower and differences of habit. In addition to the Old English Lavender, *Lavandula spica*, there is a dwarf named *L.* Twickle Purple, which has a bright purple spike of flowers, Munstead Dwarf, Hidcote Blue, and so on. There are also varieties with pink and white flower spikes. All of these need replacement here every few years as, whether they are clipped or not, they are apt to die off in patches and become unsightly with age. Heel cuttings, taken off the plants in July and put round the edge of a pot of sandy soil, are quite easy to root.

There is no prettier silver-foliaged plant than the Lavender Cotton, *Santolina chamaecyparissus* (*S. incana*) if it is well grown. Most people —count me in—let this plant straggle about from year to year, whereas if it is clipped to shape annually in the spring and renewed, say every three or four years, there is no better small shrub in the garden. A more compact form is *S. c. nana*, but I must confess that I have not tried this yet. The Lavender Cotton is evergreen, which is a useful point to remember when considering foliage contrasts in relation to winter effect. Taking cuttings is simplicity itself. In mid-summer just pull off 2-inch pieces with a heel attached and they will strike quickly in a pot of sandy soil. It is as well to nip out the tips of the newly rooted plants prior to planting them in their permanent positions.

The use of polythene has made propagation much simpler than it used to be and we are often advised to enclose our pots of cuttings in polythene bags suspended on short canes and tightly secured at the base. In the case of grey-foliaged plants, however, I find that this method produces too much humidity for the soft leaves, often causing them to rot, and that better results are obtained when the bags are left loose at the foot, allowing the moisture to escape.

Artemisia abrotanum—Old Man or Southernwood are its popular names—is not particularly silver, but I grow it for sentimental reasons and because I like its smell when it is pinched. For foliage effect its relative *A. maritima canescens* is far superior, building itself up into what is described as a cloud of silver filigree. The Old Woman or Dusty Miller, *A. stelleriana*, is a first-rate silver plant, but grows terribly straggly, as do the other two of this very hardy trio and, from a cultural standpoint, should be treated like the santolinas.

Several years ago I was given some cuttings of a fine and valuable 'silver' plant, the deeply cut foliage of which is extremely effective in floral arrangements. As it is a straggling plant reaching to about 2 feet in height, it does it no harm to shorten the growths for this purpose. I have recently discovered it to be *Senecio leucostachys*. A Patagonian sub-shrub, it is said not to be reliably hardy but it survived at the foot of a west wall for two years and was sprouting into growth for the third time before I cut it back. This operation was too much for it and it died off, but fortunately I had wintered some cuttings under glass, and I realise that I must continue to do this if I wish to maintain a stock.

My less successful shrubs include *Senecio laxifolius*. I do not mean that it is less successful because it will not grow, but rather that it is short lived. On account of this I never give it a prominent position in the garden, as in any hard winter it simply fades out, leaving an unsightly gap to be filled. If you are very fond of it, as many people are, it is as well to keep a supply of cuttings going, putting them under glass for the winter months. It is one of the easiest shrubs to root from cuttings and, like most of the greys, should be given a sandy rooting medium. This is a relative of the groundsel family, which is quite obvious when it comes into flower, with its masses of coarse, pale yellow, daisy-like blooms. Many people advocate cutting these off but I rather like them. This again is an evergreen, or rather evergrey, bush.

Salix lanata, the Woolly Willow, as the name suggests, has hairy leaves and eventually grows to about 3 feet in height. It has golden catkins in May and, while I have seen some splendid specimens of this silver-leaved shrub, I feel it will be many, many years before my 6-inch plant will give a display of any obvious charm, as it appears to be of exceptionally slow growth. My specimen of *S. boydii*, a dwarf willow which is a cross between *S. lapponicum* and *S. reticulata*, is now 2 inches in height and has been put into the rock garden before it is accidentally annihilated, and I think that this is really the best place for both of these willows.

The hardiest of the Daisy Bushes, *Olearia haastii*, an evergreen with shiny green leaves, white-felted beneath, often looks silvery, but was eventually thrown out, as it lost half of itself in every severe winter and never looked effective. There were several large bushes in the garden when we came here, but as they grew so slowly during the period in which I had them under observation, I do not think they could have been small plants when they were first put in. Of course the olearias are more fitted for maritime climates and I should love to be able to grow some of the choicer and really silvery ones. Speaking generally, no shrub of New Zealand or Australian origin is reliably hardy in my part of Yorkshire, south of Leeds.

In my chapter on rock plants, I have already mentioned several with silver foliage, such as *Alyssum saxatile*, saxifrage, sedum and the Cob-web Houseleek. Most members of the dianthus family have glaucous grey leaves and clumps of these will always form silvery patches in the garden. In addition to these, there are a few more plants that you may find of interest.

Anaphalis triplinervis, or the Pearly Everlasting Flower, was grown from seed obtained from Wisley. It now pops up in all sorts of places. The small whitish flowers are of the immortelle type, most useful for winter floral arrangements. This plant does not straggle in the accepted sense of the term, but just runs. What I think looks a superior form has been recently given to me, but it may be because it came from a cleaner district. I believe it is *A. margaritacea.* Both grow to about 18 inches.

The Rose Campion, *Lychnis coronaria*, has wonderful silver, evergreen foliage and is one of the most commonly seen garden plants. Once you have it you have it for always, as it never fails to seed itself freely. The usual colour of the flower is a brilliant, if rather harsh, crimson-magenta, but there is a deep crimson form, which I prefer, and a white one.

If you require a large silver giant for the back of your border, and a prickly one, the Scotch Thistle, *Onopordon arabicum*, should make you happy. This is only biennial, but you can depend upon its renewing itself by self-sown seeds and it is a most striking plant.

Oxalis adenophylla, the Wood Sorrel, is a most inoffensive little perennial, with neatly folded glaucous leaves, among which the mauvy-pink flowers appear in May. The foliage disappears so completely later on in the year that I forget I have it and am agreeably surprised to see it reappear in the spring. *Potentilla nitida rubra* is a lovely rock plant with silver leaves and, if grown in an open aspect in well-drained soil, seems to be quite hardy. It is not a plant for my low-lying garden, but my neighbour up the hill has one that is flourishing. *Sedum cauticolum* is another gem. The foliage is a richly glaucous dove grey and the tiny deep pink stars of flowers appearing in September, each with its brilliant red stamens, produce a perfect contrast.

A year or so ago I bought two plants of *Senecio* White Diamond to see whether or not it was hardy. It appears to be evergreen and looks rather like the Wormwood, *Artemisia stelleriana.* To test it I put one specimen under glass for the winter and the other in the open garden and the latter plant has proved hardy in the mild winters since experienced. In passing I may say that I experience considerable confusion in sorting out these families and wonder whether other people have the same difficulty.

If you want an exceptionally rampant silver-foliaged evergreen plant, then the Lamb's Ear, *Stachys lanata*, is your choice. No need to propagate this at regular intervals. When happy it just spreads and spreads and seeds and seeds, but it is not one of those plants difficult to eradicate when you tire of it, as for instance *Cerastium tomentosum* is, so it can be admitted to the garden with comparative safety. This is not my husband's opinion. I had the bright idea of using it as an edging to the vegetable garden, but it produced the seed crop to end all seed crops on this very fertile soil, and I was most unpopular until the whole lot was removed. It is considered good gardening practice to cut off the flower heads altogether, before they have a chance to go to seed, but some people never learn!

One of my friends tells me that I have left out one of the most striking of silver plants, *Verbascum bombyciferum* (*V.* Broussa). This biennial bears yellow flower spikes which may reach a height of 4 to 6 ft. and I have seen it growing well in my locality although I have not grown it myself.

From silver let us turn to gold. Here again among the evergreens I would mention are *Chamaecyparis lawsoniana lutea*, *C. pisifera plumosa aurea*, *Thuja orientalis elegantissima* and *T. occidentalis* Rheingold. Two more good ones are *Chamaecyparis lawsoniana stewartii* and *C. l. hillieri.* Later on in the chapter, among deciduous foliage trees, you will find *Acer japonicum aureum*, but there are two very common golden-leaved shrubs that I have omitted to mention. The first of these is *Ligustrum ovalifolium aureum*, or Golden Privet, which makes a most useful specimen bush although it does not always retain its leaves during the winter. I can remember in January seeing a plant growing in a local garden and wondering what on earth the effective splash of colour was. It took me some time to realise that it was a bush of Golden Privet. The other common one is the Golden Elder, *Sambucus nigra aurea.* To keep this in shape it should be pruned during the winter months. I had a specimen in the garden for many years but it was in a draughty position and never looked really tidy so in the end I dug it up. The Golden Elder makes no pretension to being other than deciduous.

Of the golden-leaved heathers, *Calluna vulgaris searlei aurea*, *C. v.* Spitfire, *Erica cinerea* Golden Drop, *E. c.* Golden Hue and *E. carnea aurea*, I have referred to in another chapter (page 77). These make delightful all-the-year-round patches of colour in the garden and are all the brighter if clipped over regularly. In passing I must mention that I am not very partial to the combination of golden foliage and pinky-mauve flowers, but I have not heard anyone else complain so must conclude that it is just a matter of my taste.

A very tiny plant like golden moss is *Arenaria verna aurea.* It is of the most brilliant shade of yellow, studded, in the spring, with minute white flowers. When a clump of it gets rather large it often develops a bald patch in the middle, in which event it is wise to tear it apart and start all over again. It grows happily in either sun or shade. One of my clumps is brightening a dull corner under an oak tree while others soften the outlines of the stone pathways.

An attractive member of the Dead Nettle family, *Lamium maculatum aureum*, has bright golden foliage, striped down the centre with white, and is reputed to be slow growing. In damp shade it has really got going with me and is a most popular plant. Fortunately it is easy to grow from cuttings if you do not wish to divide the stock plant.

The golden form of Creeping Jenny, *Lysimachia nummularia aurea*, is perfect for growing at the edge of the shrubbery and in other positions where ground cover is required. It will grow, like the green-leaved type, in the most impossible of situations and should be given a pat on the back for this reason alone. As it dies back completely in the winter, I find it possible to grow small bulbs among its roots, but do not give it too much encouragement as it is inclined to romp.

Among the purple-foliaged trees and shrubs that I grow are *Fagus sylvatica purpurea*, *Malus eleyi*, *M. lemoinei*, *M. purpurea*, *Cotinus coggygria foliis purpureis* Notcutt's Variety, *Acer palmatum dissectum atropurpureum*, and the purple-leaved nut, *Corylus avellana purpurea*, the descriptions of most of which you will find in other chapters.

The Bugle, by the name of *Ajuga reptans atropurpurea*, has glossy, evergreen, beetroot-coloured leaves. This plant looks effective when growing along the edges of paths or paving in association with the silver Lamb's Ear, *Stachys lanata*, or the golden Creeping Jenny, *Lysimachia nummularia aurea*, but I consider it too hearty for the rock garden.

Sedum Coral Carpet is most pleasing in its dress of bronzy hue. I have planted this hybrid in different parts of the garden with interesting results. Given plenty of moisture and shade for some part of the day, it seems to flower abundantly and the foliage loses much of its bronzy tone. Given full sun and fairly dry conditions it hardly flowers at all, but the foliage lives up more to the name of the plant.

Sedum maximum atropurpureum grows to a height of about 18 inches and is most striking with its purple foliage and flowers of pinkish-bronze. It may need staking when growing in an exposed position, but this would be well worth the trouble as it is a very good plant indeed. As

I had had difficulty in establishing it, having lost several small specimens, I made a final effort by purchasing two more, putting one into the open garden and the other under glass. In both cases I was lucky and the difference in the behaviour of the two plants has been interesting. The one in the garden has retained its upright habit, having a flower head on each terminal shoot and the normal dark purple leaves. By contrast, the plant kept in the cold greenhouse has grown more prostrate, and lateral shoots, each with a terminal flower head, have appeared right along the length of the main stems. The foliage of these is merely glaucous green and the flowers are several shades lighter in tone than the outdoor plant. The whole effect is extremely pleasing.

When I speak of variegated trees and shrubs I usually do so without much enthusiasm, as from personal choice I prefer the many tones of green, grey, copper and gold to mingle naturally, without the strident overtones of broken colour. But there are certain positions in the garden where a variegated plant can be introduced with advantage, as for instance, to lighten a dark corner.

Here again, I have already mentioned many of the variegated trees and shrubs. There are also a few variegated conifers, such as *Chamaecyparis pisifera plumosa albopicta*, *Juniperus sabina variegata* and *J. chinensis variegata*, which should be hardy enough to be planted in the North. For the more fortunate there are the less hardy but strikingly beautiful evergreen shrubs *Drimys colorata* and *Elaeagnus pungens aurea*, and how I envy you!

On the other hand, I have few reservations about the herbaceous plants with variegated foliage and should like to tell you about some of these.

Ajuga reptans variegata has evergreen silvery-green leaves, often with a flush of pink, and is the one to which I would award the palm. *A. r. multicolor* has all sorts of colours in its make up and, although different, seems to try too hard to be so, so that I am not altogether sure that I like it.

For those who admire the ordinary arabis, sometimes known as 'Wedding Cake', there is a form with gold and silver variegation, *Arabis albida variegata*. This makes a nice bright patch in the rock garden or at the edge of paving.

Eryngium bourgatii is a dwarf Sea Holly for the front of the border. It has deeply cut shiny green leaves splashed with whitish markings and even although it does not seem to be liking me very much, I will persevere with it. It grows to about 18 inches.

Hemerocallis fulva kwanso flore-pleno is a Day Lily that I have recently bought more out of curiosity than anything else. As well as having double flowers, the leaves are variegated but as the foliage had been cut back before it was sent to me, I shall have to wait until next season before I pass judgment. The variegation is, however, most definite. Of course, I love the day lilies, and can hardly wait to try some of the newer American hybrids, especially the clear yellows. Although they look well in the herbaceous border I always feel that they are better on their own somewhere where their full beauty can be enjoyed, and am planting them in the shrubbery.

The common Dead Nettle, *Lamium maculatum*, in its forms *album* and *roseum*, are useful carpeters for the rougher parts of the garden but are completely superseded, as far as I am concerned, by their relative the Yellow Archangel, *L. galeobdolon variegatum.* This plant literally prances about, its evergreen striped leaves attractive at all seasons of the year. Like a strawberry it roots as it runs, in bold arching sweeps. I have recently put a piece in one of my terra-cotta pots and it is already gushing over the edge.

Another evergreen plant of green and white is *Pachysandra terminalis variegata.* Growing in the shade of trees it is doing well, the shoots running along underground and sending up a few more stems at each thrust forward. It is said to have spikes of small whitish flowers in the spring, but so far these have not appeared. Some of my friends are greatly taken with it and it seems excellent for ground cover, growing about 9 inches high.

Having been brought up, as you may say, on the large sized Lady's Garters, *Phalaris arundinacea picta*, I was delighted to come across a smaller fitting, growing to 9 inches in height, or a third the size of the other. There seems to be much more whiteness in the leaves of the smaller plant, but do not ask me its name as both varieties appear to have the same name in different catalogues. It is a most attractive dwarf form of Ribbon Grass and one for which most gardeners could find a place.

Phlox paniculata Norah Leigh has been introduced to us with a bang. I bought this plant two years ago and am still waiting for it to get off the mark. I am growing it in the open in good loamy soil and cannot understand why it is refusing to prosper. As it looks so delightful when it is growing well, I will try a little coddling in the shape of some animal manure, although I am sure that I incorporated bonemeal with the soil when I put it in.

I am whole hearted in my admiration of another variegated plant that I saw growing in the grounds of the Northern Horticultural Society at Harlow Car, Harrogate. This is a member of the Figwort family, *Scrophularia nodosa variegata*, with striking leaves liberally splashed with white. It is said to be evergreen but so far I have been unable to obtain a root. *Sedum telephium variegatum* is another plant, growing to about 12 inches in height, that has recently caught my eye, as has the variegated form of the Solomon's Seal, *Polygonatum multiflorum*. Fortunately I have already secured the first but find the second in short supply. This does not surprise me as it is really beautiful.

The hostas are wonderful foliage plants, with leaves resembling the weed plantain, which accounts for their common name of the Plantain Lily. They will grow in any garden without the slightest attention, but do appreciate shade and moisture. The varieties are numerous and the one that seems to have the most popular appeal is *Hosta fortunei albopicta*. The leaves unfurl in the spring with splashes of green on a backcloth of gold. It is a most effective plant when used as a foil for evergreens and I have recently planted a border of it in the foreground of a row of Irish yews. In time this will be a permanent feature requiring no attention at all. *H. f. albopicta* is at home in the shadiest of corners and is indisputably the gayest member of the family.

Hosta glauca is equally magnificent if you are fortunate enough to be able to find it in its best form. I have bought three separate plants under this name from three different nurserymen, without any success. At last, out of pity, I was given a piece of the plant I was seeking. Showing it very proudly to my mother, who also loves gardens, I was horrified to hear her say, 'Why, it just looks like a Savoy cabbage.' Do not be put off. It is a beautiful plant at its best and, indeed, now I come to look at it through other eyes, I see that the huge leaves are of the same hue as the Savoy cabbage.

There are many other hostas, including *lancifolia*, *fortunei*, and *albomarginata*, the latter a pretty enough plant with white-edged foliage, but my favourites are the two that I have described in so much detail. Once you have become enthusiastic about hostas in general, you will not be satisfied until you have a representative collection. Some people complain that their plants are ruined by slugs and snails, but so far I have not had any bother.

The Plantain Lilies are excellent weed smotherers. To try to divide an old clump is almost as difficult as trying to break up a piece of concrete with a fork. Rather than tackle an old plant, I have a reserve of smaller plants and keep dividing these when I wish to increase my stock.

There are many other variegated plants among the pulmonarias, vincas and so on which I have described in greater detail in the chapter on herbaceous perennials. Variegations are always cropping up in the garden and I often think I will try to 'fix' them. This year I had a wonderful golden variegation on a phlox plant, but immediately I took the shoot off in an attempt to strike a cutting, it reverted to green!

The longer you garden the more you become interested in foliage as such. In speaking of foliage, my immediate thoughts are of the maples. You will all have seen those small trees with finely cut leaves which bear the name of *Acer palmatum dissectum*. In my area they can best be described as small shrubs rather than as trees. For a long time I grew a few plants in pots, leaving them in a cold greenhouse during the winter and bringing them into the house in the summer. When they become too large for their pots I put them in a sheltered raised border in the garden where I am still able to enjoy at eye level the beauty of their exquisite leaf patterns. In the autumn the foliage assumes all the brilliant colouring of a parrot's feathers, scarlet, orange and bright yellow. Admittedly they are somewhat expensive, as they are grafted, but if you have struggled with these maples as long as I have, you will think that they are worth every penny of what you may be asked to pay.

Over the past few years I have been growing acers from seed. If this is not sown immediately it is ripe, you may expect to wait a year before it germinates, but if you have some of your own seed that you can sow in the autumn, it will germinate the following spring. Now, assuming that you have a pot full of seedlings, how do you go about keeping them alive? Several times I had potted my young plants on, but found that both the ones I gave away and those that I retained died within the space of a few years. As I do not like my expectations dashed regularly to the ground, I began to seek cultural hints from those more expert than myself, but gardening is such a devious art that even the most knowledgeable can only suggest. I was advised to put half of my seedlings under glass for the winter, a procedure I had already followed, and the other half into the open garden. After much deliberation I finished up by putting the whole of my last batch into the garden where most of them, to my astonishment, survived the severe winter of 1962. One or two of them succumbed to bark split but the remainder grew strongly this season. They are not out of the wood yet and only time will tell what will happen to them in the future. Eventually the mature *Acer palmatum dissectum* should reach 7 feet in height, forming a symmetrical dome shape. They are all very lovely trees whatever the colour of their foliage. Personally I am fond of the plain green variety, *A. p. dissectum*, although if you like variegation with a suggestion of pink, there is *A. p. dissectum roseo-marginatum* or, if you prefer a dark bronzy-crimson leaf, *A. p. dissectum atropurpureum*.

Acer palmatum itself is a larger and more vigorous tree than the *A. p. dissectum* varieties. *A. p. dissectum atropurpureum* is the most popular bronzy-crimson form, growing slowly here. The colour of the foliage is most variable and I would recommend a personal selection at the nursery. Much has been written of the painfully tongue-twisting variety *A. p. heptalobum* Osakazuki. This has made a good small tree which colours well in the autumn. It comes freely from seed and does not take too long to make a sizeable plant. Do not expect it to assume its autumn tints the first season. It is one of the may or may nots so abundant in gardening. First get it to live, and then have the patience to wait.

Another choice maple of exceedingly slow growth is *A. japonicum aureum*. No words of mine can describe the beauty of the young leaves of this exquisite small tree, nor yet their texture. They emerge from their buds as a fan might unfold, each section gradually straightening out until the butter-yellow leaf reaches its full extent. One year we had a severe late spring frost just as the young foliage had emerged from the protection of its buds and, to my shocked horror, it had become completely transparent. Doing what we are always told to do in the circumstances, I fetched a can full of water and sprinkled it over my maple, which I then covered with newspaper. Fortunately the sun was not shining. A friend of mine, to whom I recounted my tale of woe, accompanied me to the spot some two hours later. Removing the newspaper rather in the manner of a conjurer producing a rabbit from a hat, no one was more astonished than I to find that the leaves had assumed their normal condition.

One of the most wonderful of all the maples is *Acer griseum*, or the Paper-bark Maple. I have grown this species from seed but realise that

I have left it far too late if, indeed, it will ever grow to any size at all here. So I must be content to look at the specimens in other gardens and hope that, in the next world, I may be granted the wisdom to give it priority.

The Snake-bark Maples have olive green bark with white striations, from which they take their name. I grow *A. hersii* and *A. davidii* and they are doing well. My *A. hersii*, grown from seed about 10 years ago, is as many feet high, while the *A. davidii* is growing at about the same rate. The foliage of both colours well in the autumn.

There is one maple which looks extremely plain once it is in leaf but which for two weeks when the foliage first unfolds has such an unusual colour effect that it is worth a place in any garden in which the owner happens to be fond of azaleas, as it blends with them so well. The name of this tree is *A. pseudoplatanus brilliantissimum* and it is exceptionally slow growing, surprisingly so when you consider that it is a variety of the common sycamore, a tree that will grow anywhere. It is also expensive, as it is grafted, but what you dislike about the price will be compensated for by the pleasure given by the leaves when they unfold in their coral-pink beauty early in the year.

Another maple which has not made much headway since it was planted is *A. nikoense*. This Japanese species is reputed to be slow growing and has certainly proved to be so. The trifoliate leaves assume the most wonderful shades of orange-scarlet before falling in the autumn. I now realise that I have planted my tree in the wrong position but feel it is too late to rectify the mistake. *Acer spicatum*, the Mountain Maple, which I grew from seed several years ago, is growing into a well-shaped erect specimen and I shall be interested to see how long it will take to reach its ultimate height of 25 feet.

One final sentence about maples in general. They do not like the wind, neither do they like the burning sun; they incline to a peaty soil, so if you admire them cherish them.

It would be foolish in a chapter on foliage effects not to touch on the subject of autumn colour. Although my part of Yorkshire is such an unpromising gardening area, there is no doubt at all that our autumn tints are just as gorgeous as those in any other part of England. This subject is far from completely understood and the colour of autumn foliage is thought to be controlled not only by the soil, but by many other factors such as temperature and rainfall. While my garden has not been planted with autumn tints especially in mind, it manages to produce them to good effect, particularly at the end of a warm, dry summer. In cases where the colours are particularly good, you will find that I have mentioned them in the text.

PLANTS REFERRED TO IN THIS CHAPTER

Name	*Origin of species*	*Ultimate height*	*Description*
Acer			
davidii	China	30–40ft.	One of the Snake-barked Maples. Bark striped with white.
griseum	„	20ft.	Extremely beautiful trifoliate leaves. Peeling bark to reveal orange-red trunk.
hersii	„	20–30ft.	Another Snake-bark Maple. Greenish bark with white striations.
japonicum aureum		15ft.	Of slow growth but has wonderful golden 7- to 11-lobed leaves.
nikoense	Japan	30ft.	Trifoliate leaves. Delightful autumn colour.
palmatum dissectum		7ft.	Dome-shaped small tree with deeply cut 7- to 11-lobed leaves. Green foliage.
atropurpureum		7ft.	Bronzy-crimson foliage.
roseo marginatum		7ft.	Slightly variegated cream and pink.
heptalobum Osakazuki		20ft.	Brilliantly coloured foliage in the autumn.
pseudo-platanus brilliantissimum		15–20ft.	Young foliage coral pink. Of extremely slow growth.
spicatum	N. America	25ft.	Autumn colour orange and scarlet.
Ajuga reptans			
atropurpurea		6in.	Bronzy-purple foliage, blue flowers, May/July.
multicolor		6in.	Leaves variegated bronze, rose and cream. Blue flowers.
variegata		6in.	Green leaves variegated with cream tinged rose. Bright blue flowers.
Alyssum saxatile	E. Europe	9–12in.	Deep yellow flowers, April/June.
Anaphalis			
margaritacea	N. America	1–1½ft.	Grey foliage, white everlasting flowers, August.
triplinervis	Himalaya	1–1½ft.	Grey foliage, white everlasting flowers, August.
Arabis albida variegata		6–9in.	Foliage variegated with yellow and silver. White flowers, spring.
Arenaria verna aurea		Prostrate	Bright yellowish-green carpeting plant. Small white flowers in the spring.

Name	Origin of species	Ultimate height	Description
Artemisia			
abrotanum	S. Europe	2–3ft.	The Southernwood. Fragrant greeny-grey foliage.
maritima canescens	Europe	1–2ft.	Delightful silver-grey foliage, finely cut.
stelleriana	N.E. Asia, E. North America	1–2ft.	Straggling grey foliage plant.
Calluna vulgaris			
searlei aurea		1½ft.	Golden foliage. White flowers, August/September.
Spitfire		1ft.	Golden foliage with mauve flowers.
Cedrus atlantica			
glauca		90ft.	Blue-grey glaucous foliage.
Cerastium tomentosum	S. and E. Europe	9in.	Snow-in-Summer. Grey foliage and white flowers. Rampant relative of our native chickweed.
Chamaecyparis			Glaucous grey False Cypress.
lawsoniana allumii		30–40ft.	Feathery grey pyramids.
fletcheri		12–15ft.	Glaucous blue.
glauca Spek		30–35ft.	Silvery-grey in summer.
hillieri		15ft.	Feathery golden cypress.
lutea		30–50ft.	Good pale golden-yellow.
Silver Queen		30–50ft.	Silvery-white in early summer.
stewartii		40–50ft.	Yellow foliage in summer, green in winter.
Triomphe de Boskoop		40–50ft.	Blue-grey foliage.
pisifera plumosa		20–30ft.	Foliage often white at tips.
albopicta			
aurea		20–30ft.	Golden form of the Sawara Cypress of Japan.
squarrosa		8ft.	Beautiful glaucous blue foliage.
Corylus avellana purpurea		6–10ft.	The purple-leaved form of the hazel nut.
Cotinus coggygria foliis purpureis			
Notcutt's Var.		6–10ft.	Outstanding purple foliage.
Drimys colorata	New Zealand	Up to 5ft.	Evergreen leaves pale yellow-green, edged and blotched dark crimson-purple.
Elaeagnus pungens aurea		12–15ft.	Evergreen leaves margined bright yellow.
Erica			
carnea aurea		6in.	Bright golden foliage, pink flowers.
cinerea			
Golden Drop		4in.	Bright golden foliage, pink flowers.
Golden Hue		1ft.	Bright golden foliage, pink flowers.

Name	Origin of species	Ultimate height	Description
Eryngium bourgatii	Pyrenees	1½ft.	Green leaves splashed with white. Bluish flowers, June/August.
Fagus sylvatica purpurea		80ft.	The Purple Beech.
Hemerocallis fulva kwanso flore-pleno		2ft.	Remarkable striped foliage. Double orange flowers, August.
Hosta			
fortunei	Japan	2ft.	Pale lilac flowers, July.
albopicta		1½ft.	Lilac flowers, July.
glauca	,,	1½ft.	Lilac flowers, July.
lancifolia	,,	1½ft.	Lilac flowers, July/August.
albomarginata		1½ft.	Lilac flowers, July/August.
Juniperus			
chinensis variegata		Dwarf, spreading	White leaves occurring among the green.
communis compressa		1–2ft.	Charming rock garden conifer with silvery foliage.
horizontalis	N. America	Prostrate	Creeping Juniper with silvery foliage.
sabina variegata		Dwarf, spreading	Creamy-white leaves among the green.
virginiana glauca		Up to 50ft.	Silvery foliage.
Lamium			
galeobdolon variegatum		1–1½ft.	The Yellow Archangel. Variegated leaves, yellow flowers.
maculatum album		9in.	Dead Nettle with white-striped leaves. White flowers.
aureum		9in.	Golden, white-striped foliage, mauve flowers.
roseum		9in.	Dead Nettle with white-striped leaves and pink flowers.
Lavandula			
Hidcote Blue		1ft.	Grey foliage, deep purple flowers. Dwarf habit.
Munstead Dwarf		12in.	Grey foliage, deep purple flowers. Dwarf habit.
spica	Mediterranean	3–4ft.	The English Lavender.
Twickle Purple		1½ft.	Grey foliage, deep purple flowers; semi-dwarf.
Ligustrum ovalifolium aureum		10ft.	The Golden Privet.
Lychnis coronaria	S. Europe	1–1½ft.	Woolly white rosettes, crimson-magenta flowers, July/August.
Lysimachia nummularia aurea		2in.	The yellow-leaved form of Creeping Jenny.

Name	*Origin of species*	*Ultimate height*	*Description*
Malus			
eleyi		Up to 25ft.	Purple-leaved Crab. Pink flowers, April/May.
lemoinei		Up to 25ft.	Purple-leaved Crab. Pink flowers, April/May.
purpurea		Up to 25ft.	Pink flowers, April/May.
Olearia haastii	New Zealand	8ft.	Glossy green leaves white-felted beneath. White flowers, July/August.
Onopordon arabicum	Europe	4–5ft.	The Scotch Thistle. Striking biennial silver-foliaged plant.
Oxalis adenophylla	Chile	3in.	Pretty greyish leaves; mauvy-pink flowers, May.
Pachysandra terminalis variegata	Japan	6–9in.	Variegated evergreen carpeting plant. Greenish-white flowers, April.
Phalaris arundinacea picta		2–3ft.	Gardener's Garters. Striped grass.
Phlox paniculata Norah Leigh		2–3ft.	Variegated form of the common garden phlox. Most attractive.
Picea pungens kosteriana		30–40ft.	Koster's Blue Spruce. A magnificent bluish form.
Polygonatum multiflorum variegatum		2–4ft.	A variegated form of Solomon's Seal.
Potentilla nitida rubra		3–4in.	Silver foliage and pink flowers in July. Not easy.
Pyrus salicifolia pendula		15–25ft.	The Willow-leaved Pear. Silver foliage.
Salix lanata	N. Europe	2–3ft.	Pretty silver-leaved shrub with catkins in May.
stuartii	„	2–3ft.	Another striking small willow with silver foliage.
Sambucus nigra aurea		15ft.	The Golden Elder.
Santolina			
chamaecyparissus	S. Europe	1½–2ft.	The Lavender Cotton. Useful silver-leaved foliage shrub.
nana		8in.	A dwarf form.
Scrophularia nodosa variegata		2ft.	Variegated Figwort. Dark green leaves variegated with yellow. Striking.
Sedum			
cauticolum	Japan	4in.	Attractive dove grey leaves; deep pink flowers, August/September.
Coral Carpet		4in.	Bronzy leaves; flesh tinted flowers, July/August.
maximum atropurpureum		1½ft.	Dark purple foliage; pinkish-bronze flowers, August.
telephium variegatum		1ft.	Green foliage splashed golden-yellow.

Name	*Origin of species*	*Ultimate height*	*Description*
Senecio			
laxifolius	New Zealand	4ft.	Grey foliage, yellow daisy-like flowers in summer.
leucostachys	Patagonia	2ft.	Deeply cut greyish-white leaves. A striking foliage plant. Pale lemon flowers, July/August.
White Diamond		1–2ft.	One of the brightest silver foliage plants.
Stachys lanata	Caucasus to Persia	1ft.	Lamb's Ear. Woolly white foliage and pinky-mauve flowers, July.
Thuja			
occidentalis Rheingold		3ft.	Dwarf conifer with golden foliage in summer, bronze in winter.
orientalis elegantissima		9ft.	Dwarf conifer with bright glossy golden foliage. Bushy, upright habit.
Verbascum bombyciferum	Asia Minor	4–6ft.	Biennial plant with striking woolly silver foliage and yellow flowers.

Conclusion

Sweet are the thoughts that savour of content;
The quiet mind is richer than a crown;
Sweet are the nights in careless slumber spent;
The poor estate scorns fortune's angry frown:
Such sweet content, such minds, such sleep, such bliss,
Beggars enjoy, when princes oft do miss.

Robert Greene

And so I have introduced you to the occupants of my garden. I hope that you have enjoyed meeting them as much as I have enjoyed describing them and that you have met some of them for the first time. I also hope that if you garden in an industrial area you will be helped by my experiences.

You may have noticed my repeated grumbling about the difficulties of gardening in a frost-hole, and certainly I do not think that there can be a worse problem. Heavy waterlogged clay can be drained and soil can be improved, but there is nothing more defeating than climate. To illustrate my point, there are two enormous ash trees growing at the streamside at the foot of my garden. When we first came here they were in magnificent health and made a wonderful background to the garden. Then disaster struck in the shape of a succession of late spring frosts. As every countryman knows, the ash tree is one of the last trees to come into leaf, in spite of the jingle about the oak and the ash. The young foliage of these trees was blackened and, in consequence several branches died right back, leaving the trees with gaunt limbs outstretched.

I could have written an equally lengthy book about plants and trees that have refused to grow here, but that would have been discouraging and, anyway, gardening is not intended to be taken too seriously. Many of the shrubs I am unable to grow are quite hardy in slightly more elevated and exposed situations, but the drawback may then be wind. A fine view from a hill-top may please, but an enthusiastic gardener prefers to huddle on more protected slopes.

Occasionally we frost-hole dwellers experience breath-taking scenes of incredible beauty. One year it was so cold for two days and two nights that the hoar frost on the trees and shrubs continued to extend until it was at least an inch-and-a-half long. The hollow lay hushed in a white embrace. Not a breath of wind stirred and a light haze threw the stark whiteness of the suspended needles of frost into sharp relief, giving the fairy-like touch of a pantomime scene. The thin fingers of the winter sun breaking through the mist shattered the enchantment, the memory of which must always persist in my mind.

If we have no experience of gardening to begin with, there is a lot of fun to be had in acquiring it, although the learning is a long and often painful process. Now that my garden is growing up I am becoming more and more daring in the plants that I try. My latest idea is to buy a few of the more reputably tender shrubs each year and, when they arrive in the autumn, pot them up and keep them under glass in a cold greenhouse for the winter. If still alive, they can then be propagated the following season and one or two of the new plants, if not the old ones themselves, put into the open garden. This means that I have an opportunity of examining the foliage and the flowers and it teaches me to recognise the type in other gardens. After all, a bundle of dormant sticks in the autumn that refuses to break into growth in the spring is not in the least informative, but a dead loss in the truest sense. In very hard winters even this method is not infallible as often the soil and roots become frozen in the pots, causing the plant to die. What has surprised me as much as anything has been the sudden death of such shrubs in late February or early March, after a very thrifty appearance during the whole of the winter. Can it be that plants, too, suffer from loss of vitality during the early months of the year?

I have also been amazed at the difference in plant behaviour within very small areas. Given six similar plants put in six different places in the garden, you will almost always get six different results as to habit and rate of growth. It is not surprising, therefore, that plant behaviour is so variable in different localities. What I am trying to say in other words is that, given the right conditions, any plant will grow anywhere and the fun in gardening lies in trying to find out what are the right conditions! No one seems to know all the answers and there you have the secret of the fascination of growing plants. It is as mystifying as the alchemist's quest for the formula for gold. It explains the donkey-like enthusiasm of the plantsman to try to grow the most seemingly impossible plants. It is the secret of individuality.

For my part it has been of help to ascertain the country of origin of the plants I would like to grow. For instance, those from Chile, Mexico and the Mediterranean are hardly likely to enjoy the Yorkshire coal-fields. On the other hand, the yucca, which hails from the coast regions of the south-eastern United States, is completely hardy and has been growing here for over 25 years. There are, therefore, no set rules. What I would advise is, first build the framework of your garden from plants known to be reliably hardy in your own area and then have fun experimenting with the unknown. Again, give your plants the best possible opportunity to prove themselves, in the way of good soil preparation, drainage and aspect. Try to find the right plant for the right place and the best variety of it. It is no good filling a garden with third-rate material when the first rate will grow equally well. And, above all, grow the plants you like yourself and not the ones people think you should.

When you have decided upon what you would like to grow, try to give as much thought to the arrangement of the material in your garden, having regard to such details as foliage and colour contrast, as you do to the arrangement of the furniture in your home and the colour schemes in it. Much pleasure may be derived from an association of silver and reddish foliage. A purple-leaved maple, such as *Acer palmatum atropurpureum*, planted in the foreground of a Blue Atlantic Cedar, *Cedrus atlantica glauca*, or *Santolina chamaecyparissus* with *Cotinus coggygria foliis purpureis* Notcutt's Variety, would give unfailing delight.

On a smaller scale, the bright golden variegated leaves of *Hosta fortunei albopicta* with a background of dark Irish yew, *Aster* Winston Churchill planted in association with *Rudbeckia speciosa*, *Cytisus kewensis* with *Androsace sarmentosa*, or *Erica carnea* Springwood Pink with *Pulmonaria angustifolia*, are equally satisfying. Even in the smallest of gardens experiments may be made in the arrangements of the material with the happiest of results.

On re-reading this volume I find that I am constantly being 'amazed', 'horrified', 'surprised' or 'delighted' by the 'pretty', 'magnificent', 'delightful', 'beautiful', 'charming', 'dainty', 'lovely', 'delicious', 'good-tempered' plants I have described. In fact I sound like a writer of journalistic puffs, so please forgive me. Primarily I am engaged in growing plants. If I have conveyed some of the enthusiasm I feel for my subject to you, then I am satisfied and hope that I will be excused for the limitations of my emotions and my adjectives.

Gardening in my part of industrial Yorkshire, I can only conclude with an excerpt from the works of John Donne which I feel sure was written specially for me:

> Little think'st thou, poore flower,
> Whom I have watch'd sixe or seaven dayes,
> And Seene thy birth, and seene what every houre
> Gave to thy growth, thee to this height to raise,
> And now doest laugh and triumph on this bough,
>   Little think'st thou
> That it will freeze anon, and that I shall
> To morrow finde thee falne, or not at all.

Index

Abbreviations:—d = line drawing, p = photograph facing page given